"Author Jennifer Watson shares how to leave behind the pain and embrace supernatural peace once and for all in her new book, *Freedom!* No matter where you are on the path to wholeness, this book will comfort, equip, and challenge you to keep pressing forward, past heartbroken to totally healed."

—Michelle Medlock Adams, award-winning and bestselling author

"We all struggle with pain from our past. Places where brokenness continues to cut deep into the fabric of our soul. *Freedom!* showcases how brokenness is not our destiny but instead is the very thing that can lead us into a deeper experience of freedom in Christ."

—Dr. Michelle Bengtson, board-certified clinical neuropsychologist, international speaker, and author of the award-winning *Hope Prevails: Insights from a Doctor's Personal Journey through Depression* and the companion *Hope Prevails Bible Study*

"Jennifer Watson is both funny and deeply rooted in faith, a combination that makes this book both fun to read and liberating. She invites us to take a gutsy look at those things that keep us from living free, and cheers us on as we find the freedom Christ offers. I highly recommend this book and the woman who wrote it."

—Suzanne Eller, ECPA bestselling author, international speaker, and cohost of *More Than Small Talk*

"Life can be cruel—full of broken dreams and gut-wrenching pain—but Jennifer Renee Watson reminds us of the wonderful truth that breakdowns are often opportunities for our greatest breakthroughs. Every tear we cry, every heartache we face is a chance to grow closer to God and become who He made us to be. As you work through the pages of this book, you'll discover helpful ways to leave your hurt behind in exchange for the faith, freedom, healing, and unending joy Christ died to give you."

—Lauren Gaskill, author, speaker, and founder of She Found Joy

"Jennifer Watson's words are a battle cry, manifesto, and life-changing invitation for any woman who's ever felt stuck in her brokenness. Her relatable style, scriptural stories, and heartfelt, practical application make Jennifer a friend and guide who will take you to a new place of greater joy, healing, and, of course, freedom!"

—Holley Gerth, bestselling author of *What Your Heart Needs for the Hard Days*

"Jennifer Renee Watson knows brokenness and beauty. She eloquently and powerfully shines a light on the messiness of life and the trauma many of us experience. Her story of holding on to hope, clinging to a God who redeems, and pushing through to a breakthrough will inspire, encourage, and provide a love letter of encouragement to every reader. This book is not to be missed."

—Jenny B. Jones, award-winning author of *In Between* and *Engaged in Trouble*

"We *all* have issues, don't we? But Jennifer Watson declares, 'our tears aren't just battle marks, they are how warriors are made.' With fiery wit and southern-girl class, Jennifer is the ride-or-die friend we all need who pushes us to find true freedom in Christ. Ready to live beyond brokenness? Read this now."

—Sarah Philpott, PhD, award-winning author of *Loved Baby: 31 Devotions Helping You Grieve and Cherish Your Child After Pregnancy Loss*

FREEDOM!

FREEDOM!

the gutsy pursuit of breakthrough and the life beyond it

JENNIFER RENEE WATSON

BETHANYHOUSE
a division of Baker Publishing Group
Minneapolis, Minnesota

Published by Bethany House Publishers
11400 Hampshire Avenue South
Bloomington, Minnesota 55438
www.bethanyhouse.com

Bethany House Publishers is a division of
Baker Publishing Group, Grand Rapids, Michigan

Printed in the United States of America

Library of Congress Cataloging-in-Publication Data
Names: Watson, Jennifer Renee, author.
Title: Freedom! : the gutsy pursuit of breakthrough and the life beyond it / Jennifer Renee Watson.
Description: Minneapolis : Bethany House, a division of Baker Publishing Group, 2019. | Includes bibliographical references.
Identifiers: LCCN 2018038576 | ISBN 9780764232701 (trade paper) | ISBN 9781493417315 (e-book)
Subjects: LCSH: Christian women—Religious life.
Classification: LCC BV4527 .W367 2019 | DDC 248.8/43—dc23
LC record available at https://lccn.loc.gov/2018038576

Cover design by Brand Navigation

Author is represented by the Blythe Daniel Agency.

19 20 21 22 23 24 25 7 6 5 4 3 2 1

To Whitley and Elise,
my favorite Gutsy Girls.

Contents

Foreword

I SAT HUNCHED on my kitchen floor, my head between my knees and shoulders thrashing as the tears flowed—my heart broken in a hundred ways.

Somewhere deep down I knew I was still a daughter of the King even in my brokenness and shattered plans. I knew God still had good plans for me, and I knew He'd already paid the price for my healing. But from my tearstained puddle on the kitchen floor, I simply didn't know how to get there.

Freedom! is the manual how.

Jennifer Renee Watson manages to pry the pity party out of the paws of her readers with the gentle nudge of a mama's heart. She tells truths that would sound hard if said by anyone else, yet Jen makes you feel like you're sitting at her breakfast nook eating blueberry pancakes smothered in sweet, sticky syrup.

And the best part? You leave her table brave, empowered, and equipped.

Please hear this truth: Your life is too valuable to be stuck. We need you at your best! The world needs your unique gifts and talents, and it's up to you to take the hand offered to help you get up and on your way again.

I know what it feels like to be paralyzed by fear, crippled with pain, and wondering if true recovery is really possible.

I join with Jen and scream a resounding YES! It is possible. The price for our healing has already been paid, although sometimes it's hard work to get our feelings and emotions aligned with God's truth.

In *Freedom!* Jen writes as a teacher, a coach, an advocate, and a soldier, charging along beside you as you begin your journey of freedom.

Let's get you unstuck—and on your way to the big plans God surely will not fail to accomplish in you.

—Shauna Shanks, author and speaker

Introduction

EACH PAINFUL MOMENT in our lives can lead to some kind of breakthrough. But most of the time, we give up right before our life-changing breakthrough happens. Why? *Because this is when it hurts most.* True breakthrough, however, is hope moving forward even when life hurts. The moment that hurts and cuts you to the core can be your starting place toward the ultimate destination: wholeness of soul.

God never wastes our pain, and He sees us like no one else can—whole and wholly His. Brokenness is not our destination; wholeness is. No matter what we have been through in life, ***the Holy Spirit will always be more powerful than the moments that try to break us.***

Stay with me—I'm trying to imagine what you look like right now. I wonder if you just nodded your head in affirmation, or if you are trying your best not to cry. Perhaps everything you are feeling right now spilled out and ruined your mascara. Maybe you want to run but your heart is telling you to dig in your heels. You are safe in feeling everything, and you are brave enough to keep turning pages. My most life-changing breakthrough was right after my biggest breakdown. Freaking out seemed like the natural thing to do when I found myself in the middle of a wild storm without an umbrella. But what I thought would leave me beyond repair actually taught me to not back down until I had a breakthrough that changed me from the inside out.

Our Biggest Breakthrough Often Comes Right After a Soul-Crushing Breakdown

I've heard it said before that most people spend their adulthood trying to get over their childhood. At one time, I was sure this would be my fate; with my long list of inner scars and insecurities, I could spend a lifetime trying to work through them. But I have learned that our messiness is often the precursor for the miraculous move of God in our hearts, relationships, and circumstances. We all have a story, and a majority of our stories are messy ones, but each can lead us to the intersection of breakthrough and letting go. Hope is just around the corner, but it's going to hurt a little before you reach your destination.

Often, when we remember our pain, we see faces of people from our past or present attached to that pain. My pain had a face, too, just like yours might now. My relationship with my father had been a source of heartache for most of my life. I spent my childhood hoping that if I prayed hard enough and was a good girl, my dad would come to love Jesus the way I did. As a teenager, I struggled with the embarrassment of being the daughter of a hot-tempered man with a drinking problem. As a grown woman, I realized I couldn't have a healthy relationship with an unhealthy person. I became aware that I couldn't fix or heal him, but I could be present in my own pain and ask God to heal the things that were broken inside of me.

Three years ago, when my father passed away, I wondered if the pain of not being able to mend our broken relationship would be a permanent sting. I wondered if I would place blame and tell myself that I hadn't tried hard enough. These questions and more were answered in a small room that held his lifeless body at the funeral home. Standing at his side, all the good things we experienced together rose to the surface of my heart. As I told him good-bye, his face no longer looked like pain to me. It looked like peace.

If your pain doesn't have a face, perhaps it is connected to a place.

Often, returning to the scene of the crime, so to speak, inflicts deep pain. Reminders and anything that resembles the trauma or hurt can cause old wounds to open. But the power of God inside of you is stronger than any face or place that tried to break you. You might feel like this is a breaking point and a line you are not ready to cross. But this is where you find the holy roar inside of you. It is already there deep within you, and when you unleash it, it's going to make the enemy wet his pants. God does not raise up victims—He leads the wounded to victory. He calls the timid ones in hiding "mighty warriors" not because of where they are in the present, but because of where they will be in the future by His power (Judges 6:12).

The tragic ending and loss of my father led me to a greater understanding of what spiritual breakthrough is all about. But this wasn't my first tragic ending. There had been a string of other devastating outcomes in my life that I had to navigate through, as well. Insecurities from not feeling good enough used to be a constant companion of mine; I often based my worth on performance or on the response of others. Lies from verbal abuse rang in my ears; I was a puppet on a string, a dog jumping through hoops—and miserable until I found my identity in

Christ. Before my father's death I was no stranger to loss. I had experienced multiple miscarriages and learned how to wait on God with an aching heart.

Yes, each moment was brutal and heartbreaking, but it was also liberating to have the proof deep within me that I had been pieced back together in such a way that I could handle whatever life throws my way because of God at work inside of me. This girl had moved forward! Each painful thing in my life led me to personal breakthrough, and each moment I was given a supernatural peace that helped me to keep going.

> I'm leaving you at peace. I'm giving you my own peace. I'm not giving it to you as the world gives. So don't let your hearts be troubled, and don't be afraid.
>
> John 14:27 ISV

Your pain right now might be attached to a face or place, but your healing is wrapped up in the Person of Jesus. Your breakthrough happens in the journey of finding healing in your story and stuck places; we can experience a spiritual breakthrough that alters the way we deal with heartache, both present and future. I believe this process is not simply the breaking of our hearts or going through unwanted transitions or changes in our closest relationships and lowering expectations accordingly—just in case we don't get what we want. This is about raising our God-expectations to flip through thin pages of His thickest promises that point to His faithfulness. To see moments in the Bible where God's people lost everything and questioned everything but dared to trust Him and storm through the enemy's camp because He commanded it and told them victory was on the other side of their bloody battle. They had to fight for their breakthrough just like we have to fight for ours. It wasn't only about winning their current battle; it was the assurance that with God's help, they could win the next one, too.

Together we will explore what breakthrough looks like for us with a heavenly, scriptural perspective. My prayer is not that you simply experience it, but that you live beyond it, fully aware that God has a plan for you that is purposeful. Hard things cannot halt the design God fashioned specifically for you. He will use each heartache for His glory if you let Him. Brokenness was never meant to be the leading character in our stories. It's the backstory and the catalyst that leads to breakthrough, freedom in Christ, and the unleashing of your holy roar.

The breaking becomes a pathway to lead us through hard times and being emotionally stuck. And on the other side of that hot mess emerges a very different version of you—the Holy Spirit–empowered version. Breakthrough is a decision to move past what you are facing or have faced, not in denial but in faith and determination with a Genesis 50:20 vision: "You intended to harm me, but God intended it for good to accomplish what is now being done, the saving of many lives."

For too long the enemy of your soul and mine has been distorting truth and whispering to us that we are undeserving of real freedom. It's time to silence that voice, and to do so, you and I need better tools and holy weapons for our spiritual battles. When you find freedom in Christ and experience a real breakthrough, it changes your outlook, your way of living, and who you are as a person.

When I began praying over this book and praying for you, I began asking God to heal each wound and help you to see that beyond your brokenness is advancement in freedom and wholeness that lasts. Each crisis and hard thing you face is an opportunity to experience the God of breakthrough who has already paid for your victory in full. You are not too far gone or too broken. You are in the perfect place to begin your breakthrough journey.

In this book you will find a Gutsy Girl Mandate to let you know that we are in this together, and concluding each chapter is a Truth Your Soul Needs section followed by reflective questions and a prayer to help you move forward in your journey. Your pain makes sense, but more than that, it deserves your attention. Lean in and listen to it as you read through each page. I don't have a formula, but I can see our symptoms and that there's a reason for them. I became incredibly bored with the broken-girl label I was wearing years ago, and I had a straight-up Holy Ghost breakthrough. I have the answer, not a formula. The answer is Jesus . . . and a stubborn refusal to give up until you are free and healed on the inside. Each chapter is designed to keep you moving forward and to help you realize healing and freedom is for you right now—not for later or "one day." As I share pieces of my story, it's important to know it's not about *what* we have experienced in life, it's about *how God wants to use it* to draw us closer to Him and redeem each hard thing for our good.

As we look at what the Bible has to say about breakthrough, we will see aspects of familiar characters come to life in ourselves. We will notice that Joseph (who couldn't help his birth order and suffered unfairly at the hands of his brothers before taking a high position in the land) faced crisis after crisis—from being thrown into a pit and sold by his brothers into slavery to being unjustly sentenced in prison—yet each experience led him to his divine destiny of being the king's dream interpreter and ultimately leading the kingdom. It wasn't about imprisonment; it was about placement—God's placement for Joseph at each turn and in His timing.

With each difficult circumstance in Joseph's life, it must have felt like God was taking him in the opposite direction of the

Lord's promise. Isn't that how we all feel sometimes? We feel like we are on the opposite side of wholeness. But with each crisis, we are given an opportunity for breakthrough and heavenly intervention. When we see a prison sentence, God sees an opportunity for us to be divinely positioned for the coming plan for our lives. Where the enemy tries to cripple you, God will strengthen you.

Breakthrough is coming. Are you ready for it?

Gutsy Girl Mandate

I am not stuck; I am steady.
I am not a lost cause, too much, or not enough. I am worth fighting for.
I am ready to make good use of my brokenness because God already paid for my wholeness.
I will not be the only one standing in my way.

PART 1

How Warriors Are Made

NONE OF US WALK through life unscarred. But I imagine that if we took the time to sit down face-to-face and bared our souls together, we would look at each wound with a sense of accomplishment. It's not about what happened to us; it's about how God wants to use it to draw us closer to Him and redeem each hard thing for our good. Those memories, scars, and tears aren't just battle wounds—they are how warriors are made.

1

More Issues than *Vogue*

STANDING IN FRONT of a crowded room full of teenagers with a microphone in your hand is downright terrifying. My friend had just shared her testimony with our growing youth group. Something powerful happens when God leads you away from your picture-perfect outline and you give in to the messiness of vulnerability. My friend told her story—the parts she used to hide because of shame—and pushed aside her title for a kind of relatability that gives wide-eyed teenagers whiplash. Many of them had no idea she had faced such heartache—a devastating divorce and deception by a man leading a double life. It was almost too much for them to take in. Like others in leadership, she begged to be taken down from a pedestal she never felt she belonged on. Yet there she stood with her heart in her hand and a word of hope for those who were hurting: *I have issues, too.*

After the service, a young girl came up to my friend and wrapped her lanky arms around her, then said, "Pain bonds us in ways that don't require words and makes us strange friends." This young lady understood pain more than anyone her age should. Her list of things to get over already was long enough. But this profound statement from her led me to believe she would harness each hard thing to connect with others just like her, just as my brave friend had. The enemy wanted shame to silence my friend, but instead it pointed her to her ministry to "strange friends," whose pain connected them in a special way.

The enemy of our souls would like to make us feel alone and isolated in our issues. But I believe issues began within the heart of the first woman ever created. In Genesis 1 God sculpted a world worth living in and made creatures to fill it, and then said, "Let Us make man in Our image, according to Our likeness" (v. 26 NKJV). God made man, then God made woman, and everything after that gets a little messy. Perhaps "little" is an understatement. I believe Eve was created to be the breakthrough her husband needed as a suitable helper for him (Genesis 2:18). The fall of man happened, and we blame Adam and Eve, but from that moment on Eve became the first woman to experience shame. Shame entered the Garden the moment she took the fruit, and it never left. It's still there following women around, saying, "You will always be broken. You are a mistake."

Eve introduced us to drama, and although I would really like to pull her hair when I reach heaven and throat-punch her, I'm painfully aware that we all probably would have done the same thing and felt the cold chill of shame on our naked, brand-new skin. Sometimes we cover up, as Eve tried to cover her heart and her bare skin. We cover the things that God intended to showcase, and we limit His blessings by believing we are too broken to experience the wholeness of God. We are still women created in the likeness of God, but somehow we walk through life with a critical eye and the lie, "I am not enough."

That day, with one bite of fruit, Adam and Eve knew they were bare, and they didn't like the way that felt. Shame makes us hide, just as Adam and Eve did after they disobeyed God. Shame makes us cover up our brokenness and place blame, but this doesn't erase our issues—it only multiplies them. Yes, Eve messed up, but that did not change God's ultimate purpose for her.

Do I think shame is the root of all of our issues? No. But accusations are. Anything that makes us feel like a fraud and tells us we are something less than who God intended us to be is a root that needs to be ripped out completely and replaced with truth.

Our brokenness was never meant to change who God created us to be. We are not alone in this struggle that is ultimately spiritual in nature, but our true design and purpose in life is bigger than anything we face temporarily or what we have been through in the past. I was the girl trying to cover up or excuse my issues, but when I owned them and asked God what He wanted to do with them, each one led to a different area of breakthrough.

Our breaking point is the place we meet God. What if we stopped thinking we were crazy for feeling things so intensely and started paying attention to the ache instead of numbing it?

We are all trying to get over something, though there are a handful of people who have made friends with their baggage and can't seem to let go. These women are fully convinced that something is wrong with them, and they don't feel worthy of blessings.

But women who are dealing with their issues and bringing them into the light are changing the world with their flawed, faith-filled hearts. Their wounded places become their mission field and place of service. This takes us to a new level of moving out of brokenness into breakthrough.

Insecurity is not humility, and confidence in Christ is not egotistical. Somewhere between the Garden of Eden then and in our personal gardens now, our insecurity, shame, and brokenness have become some form of humility, and we welcome it as a permanent fixture in our lives instead of recognizing it as the stronghold it has become. We wish away our messy moments, but our insecurities are opportunities for growth beyond our breakthrough, not merely setbacks that make us feel stuck.

Sure, we all have issues we have to deal with, but I believe we can move past the place where our issues control us. There is a long line of incredible women who overcame moments that would make your head spin. You are not alone. You are not the only one with more issues than *Vogue*, but I think it's time we break up with some of those issues and let them know who is boss.

What Will You Be When You Are No Longer the Broken Girl?

I think it's rare to have a circle of friends living in the same corner of the world, all in some form of leadership or ministry. But I have that. I can always tell how deep a friendship will grow after a few "new friend" dates. If we skip small talk about meal planning and confess that sometimes we like our dog more than we do our children, we're practically best friends already. My inner circle feels safe as we give each other permission to be real and vulnerable, knowing that often comes with a side dish of crazy and brokenness. Each friend of mine had a crisis (or two) in her life that caused a painful breakdown that led her to breakthrough and wholeness. We will always be friends because we know way too much about each other. You could say we are "ride or die" friends, but we are really "sit and snack" kind of girls. Beyond our fun-loving conversations and total commitment to crazy is a deeply rooted love for each other and a desire to see each one who gathers around the table living in the fullness God has for us.

Over dinner or coffee the conversation flows, and we have freedom to be shamelessly real because we are fiercely loved and accepted by our tribe. Even though we all have come so far, we still have moments when the broken girl inside of us surfaces. We *all* have our things. But we all have a choice to make. Will it become a trap for the enemy to snare us, or a noteworthy moment when God showed up as we sought Him?

Many years have passed since the following question was asked, and still I think of it like an echo:

"What will you be when you are no longer the broken girl?"

I texted my friend Keri to ask her about her response when our friend Holley asked her this question. Here is what she said:

> I don't even remember what I said. But, I can tell you who I am now. I am not a broken girl. I'm new. I'm strong and tender and confident and childlike and free. I don't feel a constant tug on me to look back anymore. It's like Jesus untied all the strings, grabbed my hand, winked, and said, "Let's go, baby girl."

As a charismatic Southern girl, I wanted to shout and wave my monogrammed hanky after reading that. Who knows what I would have said during that season years ago. Maybe I would have been silent or said, "I don't know." My guess is that I would have whispered softly one word: *unbroken*. I thought that was the ultimate goal then, but not now. I have a much different view of brokenness. I don't see it as being damaged goods or having "more issues than *Vogue*." No, none of those labels will do. Only one: grateful. Girls who have been set free and now walk in wholeness are grateful girls.

> Give thanks in all circumstances; for this is the will of God in Christ Jesus for you.
>
> 1 Thessalonians 5:18 ESV

Brokenness is not the ending; it's the beginning of something beautiful inside of you being rebuilt. It looks like gratitude rather than guilt. People can talk about what you used to be, but God is stirring something inside of you that will motivate you beyond labels of brokenness to victory and wholeness. What if when you shared your story no one could fathom it actually happened to you? And that your identity is so untethered from the past that others marvel at the goodness of God? This can absolutely happen to you; I know, because it happened to me.

The purpose of this book is not to have you mentally block your broken past; the purpose is to show you how to harness the hard things and the brokenness attached to them to find your gutsy roar. The next step of breakthrough will tell you everything. Will you move forward for good, or be the girl repeating this process for a really long time? I did the latter for far too long, and I know for a fact that it doesn't have to be that way.

It Will Get Better

You will eventually be in an emotionally healthy place, but take the time to heal even if it takes longer than you think is "normal." Do the hard work to be free, because life is too sweet to remain stuck in the past. The hard work it takes to be free begins with giving ourselves room to be okay with not being okay while believing something better is coming. That state of the heart and the pain we are feeling right now is temporary. Our progress happens when we pay attention to our heart and take time to journal, pray, and receive godly counsel. Our growth happens when we ask the Holy Spirit to help us as we explore healing and spend time in the presence of God. And our faith is exercised by looking at the truth in Scripture as our remedy, our healing salve, and our anchor when our emotions are all over the map.

Here are three truths that can anchor us when we are going through difficult times:

What I am facing is temporary.

What I am feeling is temporary.

Good things will come from this pain, even though I can't see them yet.

This is what I believe about issues: When we surrender them to God, we not only open the door to conquering them, but we also unlock the gate to our true purpose in life. Where the enemy of our soul tries to *shame* us, the power of God wants to *shine through* us. We are beacons of hope, not damaged goods. Before each breakthrough you will find a decision point: Will you keep going or shrink back?

Our issues are not meant to be limitations; they are designed to be launching pads to live more fully. We are not the first women on earth to be at war with labels and brokenness. We are some among many who decided to do the hard work of eliminating lingering damage and scars from the past and moving forward, knowing God wants to use us not in spite of those things, but because of them. This is breakthrough. I believe that labels and the lies others believe are what hold women captive today—those who remain stuck in brokenness and don't activate their breakthrough. What if our mindset is the biggest obstacle standing in our way? I believe it is!

It's time to claim breakthrough and live beyond it. Are you with me?

Truth Your Soul Needs

I dare you to ask, "God, what do you want to do with my 'More Issues Than *Vogue*' life?" I pray that you feel this answer stirring in your heart: *He wants to use it*. Those things that broke your sweet heart into a million fragmented pieces were never meant to harden you. Nope, they were meant to transform you. We can harness the hard things we face into the boldness of becoming more like Him.

Stuck girls tell the same stories. Cry about the same things. Dwell on hurts instead of on the wild pursuit of healing. Sometimes it helps to make a road map of where you want to go on this journey. When it comes to issues, it's important to put a DEAD END sign up and make a commitment to moving forward in life and not dwelling on the past.

Take a few minutes to list three motivations for moving forward:

____

____

____

Soul Destination Map

Fill out this section and create an inventory of the heart to begin your road to breakthrough. This is a time of honesty with yourself about how you are really doing and what is holding you back. I have learned that calling those things out and bringing them into the light not only brings healing but also creates a partnership with the Lord to work through those things with His help.

I need to make peace with:

I need to stop being so hard on myself about:

I need to cling to:

I need to release:

Reflective Question

What will you be when you are no longer the broken girl?

Gutsy Prayer

Lord,

I have issues and lack wisdom in this area in my life: ________________________________.

James 1:5 says that if I lack wisdom I can ask you for it and that you give it out generously. I thank you for your generous gift and trust that nothing I face takes you by surprise.

I trust in you, Lord, with all my heart. I do not lean on my own understanding. In all my ways, I choose to acknowledge you and know that you alone will make the path before me straight (Proverbs 3:5–6).

In Jesus' name, amen.

2

Gutsy Girls

SHE PRESSED THROUGH the crowd with what little strength she had left, desperate and depleted. She had forgotten what it was like to be known for who she was instead of by the sickness that now controlled her. She was a woman active in the pursuit of healing, but even that left her empty-handed and flat broke. One empty hand reaching out was all she needed, and it proved she was willing to place herself on a path to healing one more time. Too weak to run ahead of Him, she trailed behind that man she heard about named Jesus.

I get this woman because I have been her. I was the woman who couldn't carry a child to full term. I experienced two early miscarriages close together and found out that something I once thought was easy, wasn't easy for me at all. After the doctor opened me up during exploratory surgery, he later explained that the damage within looked like a war zone. I cried because he confirmed what I already knew: Something was wrong. I was diagnosed with endometriosis and went through years of treatment. During this time, I began to understand that my heart was a war zone, too, often wrestling with anxiety. But just like this woman, I refused to give up. I wonder if she thought about all the bad advice and uneducated guesses of well-intentioned people, or thought about all the things she had already tried, like home remedies and three easy steps to find the right cure to heal her inner brokenness. A huge part of me believes she left all of those empty promises behind her.

If I can reach the hem of His garment, I will be whole again. I don't even need a hand to hold; I'm beyond that. I don't need a glance in my direction or a word spoken to me. I need my hands to reach out in hope just one more time.

Here's the story of one gutsy sick girl who refused to give up.

> And a woman was there who had been subject to bleeding for twelve years. She had suffered a great deal under the care of many doctors and had spent all she had, yet instead of getting better she grew worse. When she heard about Jesus, she came up behind him in the crowd and touched his cloak, because she thought, "If I just touch his clothes, I will be healed." Immediately her bleeding stopped, and she felt in her body that she was freed from her suffering.
>
> At once Jesus realized that power had gone out from him. He turned around in the crowd and asked, "Who touched my clothes?"
>
> "You see the people crowding against you," his disciples answered, "and yet you can ask, 'Who touched me?'"
>
> But Jesus kept looking around to see who had done it. Then the woman, knowing what had happened to her, came and fell at his feet and, trembling with fear, told him the whole truth. He said to her, "Daughter, your faith has healed you. Go in peace and be freed from your suffering."
>
> Mark 5:25–34

Gutsy Faith Is Noticed and Rewarded By God

On that day, the sick girl got far more than healing; she got a new name and a place of belonging in the body of Christ. She was now called "daughter," one with a gutsy faith that made Jesus stop in His tracks. He knew who touched Him and exactly what she needed. And because she was an active participant in her healing, she trembled at His feet and told the whole truth.

It's time to get a little gutsy in the pursuit of a miracle, don't you think? I'm tired of seeing God's daughters pummeled by the enemy and listening to all the wrong voices that have left them even more confused and broken instead of whole. Your freedom journey is this: It's you reaching out to take hold of Jesus and telling your whole truth. It's you signing up to be active in your healing because your soul is worth your attention. Everything you do flows from it.

Maybe, like me, you have found yourself asking God to show you what lies you might be believing.

These labels are not who you are; they are just the place where you begin today—with empty hands reaching out to Jesus as His beloved daughter.

The truth of active brokenness: There is nothing weak about the pursuit of Jesus and the wholeness He has for us.

Soul Reflection: Hope Worth Reaching For

> And so it was that he [Abraham], having waited long and endured patiently, realized and obtained what God had promised.
>
> Hebrews 6:15 AMPC

The Holy Spirit will always be greater and more powerful than whatever tried to break you.

Our hope is found in believing that reaching out to God and seeking Him first will result in rewards for us personally that are worth waiting for. And what we are becoming in the process of waiting and reaching out is worth the effort it takes to keep going. Pressing and reaching leads us closer to our ultimate goal as believers, which is being closer to the Lord. The Bible shows us how releasing and forgetting those things behind us, all of those things we can't control—all of the missteps that make us feel like failures—to reach forward to the things ahead, is the only success that matters. This is faith and active brokenness: reaching out toward Christ to receive the wholeness our soul needs. Reaching out will always be part of our process in active faith. I know for a fact that my breakthrough began with a stubborn belief that by reaching out to God I would find Him. My persistent reaching was the catalyst I needed not only to experience a breakthrough in my life but to move beyond the stuck places in my heart and the victim mentality we can all be sucked into.

> Not that I have already attained, or am already perfected; but I press on, that I may lay hold of that for which Christ Jesus has also laid hold of me. Brethren, I do not count myself to have apprehended; but one thing I do, forgetting those things which are behind and reaching forward to those things which are ahead, I press toward the goal for the prize of the upward call of God in Christ Jesus.
>
> Philippians 3:12–14 NKJV

Reaching forward to gain all the things Christ has waiting for us and letting go of the past is pivotal in this journey. For some of us, that is easier said than done. Maybe you have a mother lode of baggage to get over; the truth is that we all do. We are not alone in this, but the punk-faced devil wants to isolate us and make us believe that for some crazy reason it's just us. That there is something wrong with us, so we are getting what we deserve. But this is a lie from the fiery pit; it's time to believe the truth in God's Word over the lies we find easier to swallow. Each time we let go of something, forgive someone, and ask for the forgiveness we need, we reach beyond ourselves to receive the grace we all long for. More grace. More love. More of the power of God flowing through us. The reaching will always be worth it. The state of your heart and soul is worth it. It's time to fight on your behalf instead of enduring self-inflicted sabotage on your soul.

Over It: Brokenness, It's Time to Take a Backseat

I was invited to a prayer meeting at my mentor's house many years ago. I was the new girl and knew only a few of the ladies, which is pretty much torture for introverts. Things began to shift inside my heart, and I knew for certain God was bringing me into a new season that looked a lot like freedom. This group of ladies had been meeting together for a decade. They were of all ages and backgrounds—and all were profoundly devoted to God but still in the process of healing. Some were further along than others.

A guest was brought in to speak to our group and then pray for us. She was tall, poised, and intentional about every word that left her mouth. And she scared me to death. I was convinced she could see right through me.

I sat in the chair knowing that God was going to read my mail, bracing myself for a much-needed spiritual spanking: I would have to deal with my tendency to run away from things instead of facing them head on. God knows that I am very relational, so I assumed He would use one strong woman to speak to the strong woman within me who had reverted to an old pattern that was holding me captive. I leaned back in my chair and listened, wanting only one thing—to remain invisible. I didn't want to be singled out, but I also didn't want to remain stuck and held back in new situations. When it came time for prayer, the speaker looked at me and said, "You're held back." Dang. It wasn't this lady who was calling me out; it was God.

Jennifer, it's time to stop hiding.

But what I couldn't figure out was why I was held back when everything in my spirit wanted to break out. Why, after all these years of progress and becoming more in Christ, did I still revert to a defeated default setting? I knew in my heart that it was because I had been hurt and had deep wounds that fragmented my identity—which was held together by insecurity and feelings of "I'm not good enough or smart enough." I firmly believed that I had received healing, so why wasn't I walking in that? Why, after all of the progress, did I still go to that dark place of *not enough*? The answer was painfully simple and had nothing to do with placing blame on anyone but myself. It was a mindset problem: We can either take our thoughts captive or be held captive by them. Ouch.

There is an epidemic sweeping throughout the hearts of women: While we have outed our brokenness and can talk about it freely, somehow brokenness has become the biggest star in our story—not the backstory or the catalyst it was meant to be. It was meant to spark a fire in our souls and light a fire to the backside of our skinny jeans to spur us to take action and change. Never has stuckness been so comfortable and easy to numb and ignore. If you don't believe me, just go back to binging Netflix. Or stay with me, because I was the queen of shutting down, comfortable with being invisible because breaking wide open hurt too dang much.

Every story ends with a resolution and the tying up of loose ends. But with believers, the resolution is restoration and wholeness in Christ. I believe it's okay not to be okay for a season. But beyond that is freedom so powerful that it deserves to take the leading role in our stories.

> There was a woman present, so twisted and bent over with arthritis that she couldn't even look up. She had been afflicted with this for eighteen years. When Jesus saw her, he called her over. "Woman, you're free!" He laid hands on her and suddenly she was standing straight and tall, giving glory to God.
>
> Luke 13:10–13 MESSAGE

He Called Her Forward, Then Set Her Free

I'm afraid that we have been walking around with bent-over and twisted hearts inside us for far too long, adopting a mindset of stuckness and a lowered posture. Jesus sees you just like He saw her. He called her forward so He could set her free. She was no longer the one with the twisted body and heart; she was standing straight and tall and giving all the glory to God.

For decades, my mindset was twisted and bent in such a way that I couldn't look up. I was stuck in a pattern of destructive thinking that crippled me and robbed me of my power in Christ. I had access to that power, but I wasn't laying claim to it like it belonged to me. I think it's time for brokenness to take a backseat and for real breakthrough that lasts to become our focus and our new normal. You can't be a victim when your hands are in the air praising God. God is in the business of restoring souls and stories. Brokenness, it's time for you to take a backseat.

> "The Lord God is my strength [my source of courage, my invincible army]; He has made my feet [steady and sure] like hinds'

> feet. And makes me walk [forward with spiritual confidence] on my high places [of challenge and responsibility].
>
> Habakkuk 3:19 AMP

Actively reaching out to Jesus in your brokenness is the precursor to the intentional letting go of things in your past. Tackling the ginormous task of forgiving yourself and others leads not only to lasting freedom, but also to real healing that lasts. Before we can move on to soul scars and what to do with those wounds that easily reopen, we can purpose in our hearts to pursue active brokenness and letting go by surrendering—not just a few things, but everything. As the verse in Habakkuk says, we walk forward with spiritual confidence instead of living in the place of doubts. We rise up in faith because that's what gutsy girls do. We always rise.

The gutsy girl with the issue of blood pursued Jesus because she knew He could heal her, so she pressed through the crowd with a purpose: to grab hold of Jesus to receive the healing she needed. Each commitment we make to pursue the God who restores and makes all things new comes from looking at our situation through faith-filled eyes instead of viewing all the evidence the enemy has stacked against us.

You, my friend, are a gutsy girl. That's why you are reading this. You are stronger than you know, and you are ready for a breakthrough that changes you from the inside out. I'm so proud of you already, so let's keep going, shall we?

Truth Your Soul Needs

- Reaching out to Jesus in your brokenness is an act of faith, not weakness.
- Gutsy faith is noticed and rewarded by God.

- You are not too far gone; you are ready to take a step of faith.
- God wants to set you free.

Reflective Questions

1. What do you need from Jesus?
2. Name the dead weight you are dragging behind you.
3. What are the labels or phrases that have become tangled up with your identity? (Mine, for example: *Recovering broken girl*, *anxiety*, *depression*, *chronic illness*, *chronic negativity*, *unable to forgive myself and others*, *recovering people-pleaser listening to all the wrong voices . . .*)

Gutsy Prayer

Lord,

I have been a woman twisted on the inside and unable to look up (Luke 13:10–13). I have been fixated on my pain instead of trusting you for my healing. I have been afflicted with a long list of things, but I believe your perfect plan for me is healing and freedom! Today I am reaching out to you and ready to receive all that you have for me.

In Jesus' name, amen.

3

Taking It Back

The Same Kind of Stuck

My friend leaned over from across the table and asked, "Why do you think so many women are held back?"

Maybe it's because *stuck* has become the norm. I tell her how I'm certain that I fell for it, too—that "I'm almost there" mindset. Yes, how far we have come is worth celebrating. But being "almost free" isn't real freedom at all. It's like finding out your "healthy smoothie" had 750 calories and an entire bag of sugar. With that many calories, it should have tasted magical and been made by unicorns—but it didn't and it wasn't. But the disappointment experienced when "almost free" doesn't deliver is far more profound than that of a fattening smoothie. Beyond the frustration is the truth that almost free is a spiritual counterfeit. It throws us off the path, making us think we are exactly where we need to be. Like shimmery bait that looks like the real deal to hungry fish, it seems promising but delivers a sharp, cold hook that is a death sentence.

The enemy wants us to pursue the wrong solutions, thinking they are the answer. Do more. Try harder. Check off all the boxes, and then add a few more. He wants us to believe that some progress is better than none at all. And if you compare yourself to others who are barely surviving life right now, you are going to feel much better about yourself. Who wouldn't? But freedom in Christ isn't having what others have or don't have; it's about thriving on the inside even when times are tremendously hard.

With almost twenty years of ministry under my belt, I can tell you with certainty that the inability to move on from the past is common with believers. I have been there with them, hurting and unable to move on, too. I understand how easily personal baggage can wound our permanent identity. But I truly believe with all my heart this is not God's plan for us. His will is to set the captive inside of us free. One of my favorite passages in the Bible reminds me that we sometimes (more often than not) return to our captivity.

> It is for freedom that Christ has set us free. Stand firm, then, and do not let yourselves be burdened again by a yoke of slavery.
>
> Galatians 5:1

We cannot continue to return to the chains of our past that once held us captive and wonder why we are miserable and stuck in the same place we were years ago, perhaps even decades ago. One of the most prominent reasons we are stuck is that we are glorifying our brokenness and are afraid to take the next steps. No one likes to rip the bandage off, but we have to. I believe we need to give ourselves permission to feel everything and grieve the hard things we face in life, but we filter those things with hope in Christ—eventually. It's okay if we don't feel hopeful at first; we can stand firm (after we freak out some) until hope returns. We are meant to feel pain and to process what we are experiencing with the promise that Jesus will be near to us.

Our scars become success stories that reflect His glory to the people around us. We trade ashes for beauty without collecting the dust that goes with them. Why would we hang on to ashes when we can have something of infinitely greater worth in our lives and hearts instead? Are you holding on to the ashes of your past? Are you ready to trade them in for what God has for you? I believe you are ready, and I know God is able, sweet friend.

Lord,

I let go of the pain and ashes of my past and the brokenness that I carry with them so I can take hold of the beauty you have for me. You give beauty for ashes, joy instead of mourning, and praise instead of despair. I choose strength instead of the fear that keeps me from taking those next steps toward you. I want joy instead of mourning, your sweet peace for despair (Isaiah 61:3). Help me to release the things in my heart that cause me to question your goodness toward me. I'm ready to trade up with you.

In Jesus' name, amen.

The Walls We Build

Our heart and mind have boundaries and Keep Out signs—roped-off places with yellow tape and bold black letters marked Crime Scene and Do Not Enter. We all have our list of wrongs. We know we are not supposed to keep score, but some of us latch on to our list like our life depends on it. We take on a label from a past soul injury and carry it with us. Even thirty years after the fact, I have watched women refuse to take off such labels and continue to collect them, wearing them like a garment that no longer fits, or a tarnished ring that has lost its sparkle.

We shut down thoughts with constant distractions and keep at arm's length people who trigger pains from the past that remain unhealed. Our baggage leaves us trapped and labeled, whether we admit it or not. But that is not how Christ intended us to live. Scripture says, "Now the Lord is the Spirit, and where the Spirit of the Lord is, there is freedom" (2 Corinthians 3:17). When this liberty comes, chains are broken, yellow tape is torn down and trashed, and a brave heart becomes borderless and inhabits a vast space that Christ paid for on the cross.

Much of what has caused you the most pain in life is something that you wish had never happened, but it did. But choosing to see something that the enemy tried to destroy you with as the advancement that God will use for your good can change everything. I know this isn't easy, and I have lived my heartache on repeat. But if I can do this, I truly believe anyone can. There is nothing special about me other than the fact that I am special to God. You are so precious to the heart of God, so why not have everything He has in store for you? What we can do to make real progress in this area is focus on rearranging those thoughts in our heart to this:

God will use this for my good and His glory, even if I can't see anything good or glorious in this right now.

The enemy meant to destroy me with this, but God intends to employ me with it.

The devastation those encounters caused results in your being "hired for service" in a specific work God has for you to do on this broken, needy earth. What the enemy meant to entangle you with, God himself will empower and equip you to overcome, and take back territory that has your name on it. But your name isn't the only one; others just like you are there waiting for their healing, too. For years you have held everything in and kept quiet, but when freedom comes, a new boldness comes with it. You will find your people and tribe—a group you can lead better than anyone else because you get it. This kind of gutsy residence and taking back stolen territory doesn't happen overnight, unfortunately. But that doesn't mean victory for you isn't just around the corner. Every day you are moving toward something; why shouldn't it be your ultimate healing and freedom?

In Genesis 50:20 we see Joseph's response to his brothers—not Satan, but his flesh and blood: "You intended to harm me, but God intended it for good to accomplish what is now being done, the saving of many lives."

Satan did, in fact, want to harm and thwart the plan of God in Joseph's life, and Satan used Joseph's brothers to do his dirty work.

It started with boys being boys and with a father loving one more than all the rest (Genesis 37:3). With the favoritism so obvious, hatred grew like cancer in the hearts of Joseph's brothers. Joseph dreamed of greatness, but later was rebuked by his father for sharing the dream. He was thrown into a pit and sold into slavery by his brothers; was chased by a man-eating, desperate housewife; and then was thrown into prison. None of this was part of Joseph's dream of greatness and importance. He had to go through hardships to wind up in a position to save his renegade brothers who needed food, a lesson in humility, and redemption.

God gave Joseph a dream, and He fulfilled it as those things came to pass, but Joseph had to overcome a lot of baggage before he got there. The question is, could Joseph have become what God intended by being the favorite, spoiled son and having everything handed to him on a silver platter, or did each heartache lead to his promotion and his greatness? I have to believe that he was everything God intended him to be because of all the painful moments.

Our pain isn't intended to destroy us; it is designed to position us for God's ultimate purpose for our life. Good things are coming your way; I've watched this become true for so many people I love, and I believe it will be the same way for you and for the ones you love. You will live beyond your breakthrough. You will take back enemy territory. You will not be forever stuck; this is merely a sticky beginning for you. Better days are coming because of the hard work you are doing right now. Gosh, I'm so proud of you.

Risky Living

Ministry is often referred to as a fishbowl, with all eyes looking in. Over the years, as I started to allow others into my life, I placed a Welcome mat at the door of my heart. I stopped worrying about ridicule and chose risky relatability instead. That risk taking has opened far more doors than carefulness ever did. I let those doors swing wide open as I made peace with the broken parts of my story. I guess I relaxed a little; maybe that is from growing older and fitting into my skin better. Either way, I'll take it.

I think there is a celebration of brokenness that says, "Hey, look at my hurts." But we are missing the nail-scarred hands and the power of the cross that point to the healing already purchased on our behalf. For some reason, we have become too timid to cash it in and move on. Maybe it's because our insecurities and our past have become tethered to the core of our identity. Perhaps we think it's easier and safer to ignore our mother lode of baggage instead of doing the hard work to get over it.

Over the years, I began asking myself some pointed questions, for example: How can God get glory from the things we refuse to get over? Ouch.

Uncluttering our heart leads to better things that last. Freedom looks like making better friends with our story, even the part of our story we used to omit, faking our way with the lie, "I'm fine." We can stop celebrating brokenness by focusing on wholeness in Christ. Sometimes our emotions can be irrational, but it doesn't stop us from feeling them. Fear is a liar. Tell it to hush so you can listen to the Holy Spirit. And our pain is never wasted space. We can face it head on, or we can default to a prettier version of pretending that leaves us stationary. But how do we become unstuck?

Becoming unstuck begins with one small step forward and a commitment to fight to continue to move forward.

When a woman says, "I'm done," it usually means, "I need you to fight for me." I have a feeling that right now, many of you feel the same way. You need someone to fight *for* you, not *with* you. But I'm going to ask you to do something for me. I need you to fight this time, knowing that you have already won the most crucial battle with every page turned. You are showing up for your life, and maybe you don't believe me right now when I tell you that you are worth that kind of fight, but you are. You are worth fighting for, and worth the effort it takes to push past opposition and doubts for the gutsy breakthrough ahead.

I don't want you to try harder; I want you to believe boldly that your breakthrough and promise from God is based on the finished work of Christ. Honey, it's already paid for—you don't have to earn it. But you do have to fight the good fight of faith for it (1 Timothy 6:12). Think mustard seed if that's all you've got right now. Start small and then turn the page and let hope grow from there. There is power when we not only believe the Word of God, but we decree it. Yeah, that sounds a little too bold, or gutsy, doesn't it? But maybe I'm on to something. If God said it, why shouldn't we believe it and wait expectantly for it?

We are taught to be nice and sweet, to say please and thank you—and we should be and do those things. But when it comes to the enemy of your soul and taking steps away from the toxic behavior all of us have to war with, nice isn't going to cut it. That's where the indwelling power of Christ comes into play. We trade our fears and insecurities for a certainty that is rock solid.

> Now to him who is able to do far more abundantly than all that we ask or think, according to the power that works in us.
>
> Ephesians 3:20 ESV

I know nice Southern girls aren't supposed to get mad or, heaven forbid, act like they are ticked off, but why not? Why can't we be ticked off about what the enemy has stolen from us? I think it's about dang time we get mad and storm enemy territory armed and ready to take back what belongs to us. I want you to look beyond what or who hurt you to know that the enemy loves to use people to inflict damage on the hearts of God's beloved. There is nothing he loves more than to turn good people against each other and have them distracted from what matters most.

> The thief does not come except to steal, and to kill, and to destroy. I have come that they may have life, and that they may have it more abundantly.
>
> John 10:10 NKJV

Battlefield: Facing Our Foes and Finding Our Destiny

A battle plays out in the hearts of God's beloved in the Old Testament. They are God's chosen people and His prized possessions, but they are still children—prone to wander and to dismiss the boundaries God put in place to keep them safe in His blessing. No one wants a spiritual spanking, but we all need one at times. But this wasn't an inner tug-of-war; it was a full-throttle, bloody battle, and one they were losing. Joshua went from being led and assisting the leader to becoming the leader after the death of Moses. No one wants to follow the golden child, yet we see God's hand in it as He commissioned Joshua to step into a role to fill some pretty big shoes. Joshua 1:1 identifies him by name, then by title: Moses' assistant.

"The Holy Spirit's work is mutual."[1] I read this profound statement in my study Bible this morning. We are not puppets on a string; we are partners. We need God's help and the work of the Holy Spirit as our helper—that's a no-brainer. And yet, that requires our stubborn faith to believe and trust God, even when the odds seem stacked against us. To take back enemy territory—meaning our favor, blessing, and position as believers—we have to recognize it was ours to start with.

> Every place that the sole of your foot will tread upon I have given you, as I said to Moses. From the wilderness and this Lebanon as far as the great river, the River Euphrates, and all the land of the Hittites, and to the Great Sea toward the going down of the sun, shall be your territory. No man shall be able to stand before you all the days of your life; as I was with Moses, so I will be with you. I will not leave you or forsake you. Be strong and of good courage, for to this people you shall divide as an inheritance the land which I swore to their fathers to give them. Only be strong and very courageous, that you may observe to do

according to all the law which Moses My servant commanded you, do not turn from it to the right hand or to the left, that you may prosper wherever you go.

Joshua 1:3–7 NKJV

Truth Your Soul Needs from the Life of Joshua

- God's blessing and favor belong to you.
- No one will be able to stand before you or against you. But that doesn't mean they won't try.
- God will be with you. When everyone else walks out on you, God will still be there.
- Your job is to be strong and courageous, to let God be God, and to stay in your lane.
- Follow His Word and you will prosper, but that doesn't mean you won't have problems and that life will be all butterflies and rainbows.

Reflective Questions

1. What hard thing is the Lord going to use for your good and His glory, even if you can't see anything good or glorious in it right now?
2. In what area of your life might a little risk taking open a door?

Gutsy Prayer

Lord,

I am not stuck; I am steadfast. I am ready. I am not emotionally unstable; I am steady and able to handle everything that comes my way because God is with me. I can do all things because you give me strength! (Philippians 4:13).

I will not be held back by the things that have happened to me. I will not dwell on anything but the faithfulness of God and things above (Colossians 3:2). You must have seen something bigger inside of me than I see in myself right now. But I choose to believe that today, right now, I am moving forward and moving on. I am living in the power of breakthrough, and from this I will find new freedom in my everyday life that nothing can stop or hinder.

In Jesus' name, amen.

Therefore, since we are surrounded by such a great cloud of witnesses, let us throw off everything that hinders and the sin that so easily entangles. And let us run with perseverance the race marked out for us.

Hebrews 12:1

4

Battle Cry

When the Sky Is Falling and People Are Cray Cray

NOTHING MAKES ME want to go from zero to postal more than when my husband tells me I'm acting crazy. I'm (painfully) aware, he just missed the warning signals that got me there. I asked the kids nicely five times; by six or seven, I'm using my "mom-voice," which is practically yelling but just a tiny bit softer. And I'm using dramatic gestures and have what they call "crazy eyes." We are wired differently, men and women, but that doesn't mean we are wired improperly. But it sure feels like it, doesn't it? We just speak a different language; I speak fluent girl, which is not his strong suit. At all.

There are rules in marriage and friendship: If we want a healthy, happy relationship, we have to learn—with tears, gnashing of teeth, and the sweat of our ancestors—to communicate in a way that the other person feels loved, safe, heard, and respected. When we spell out our boundaries clearly, things tend to go better. But what do we do when people don't listen to us? It hits the fan, right? We can easily laugh off the misunderstandings we have with one another after the dust settles and we've all said, "I'm sorry for calling you crazy." But what happens when we don't listen to and obey God? We board the Hot-Mess Express, and things get jacked up, that's what.

To set the stage, the Israelites had just crossed the Jordan River. The waters parted so they could cross to the other side safely. But then things became increasingly difficult because people are crazy and don't listen to God. Bad move. Here's what went down:

> Our Lord, did you bring us across the Jordan River just so the Amorites could destroy us? This wouldn't have happened if we had agreed to stay on the other side of the Jordan. I don't even know what to say to you, since Israel's army has turned and run from the enemy. Everyone will think you weren't strong enough to protect your people. Now the Canaanites and everyone else who lives in the land will surround us and wipe us out.
>
> The Lord answered:
>
> Stop lying there on the ground! Get up! I said everything in Jericho belonged to me and had to be destroyed. But the Israelites have kept some of the things for themselves. They stole from me and hid what they took. Then they lied about it. What they stole was supposed to be destroyed, and now Israel itself must be destroyed. I cannot help you anymore until you do exactly what I have said. That's why Israel turns and runs from its enemies instead of standing up to them. Tell the people of Israel, "Tomorrow you will meet with the Lord your God, so make yourselves acceptable to worship him. The Lord says that you have taken things that should have been destroyed. You won't be able to stand up to your enemies until you get rid of those things. Tomorrow morning everyone must gather near the place of worship. You will come forward tribe by tribe,

and the Lord will show which tribe is guilty. Next, the clans in that tribe must come forward, and the Lord will show which clan is guilty. The families in that clan must come, and the Lord will point out the guilty family. Finally, the men in that family must come, and the Lord will show who stole what should have been destroyed. That man must be put to death, his body burned, and his possessions thrown into the fire. He has done a terrible thing by breaking the sacred agreement that the Lord made with Israel."

Joshua got up early the next morning and brought each tribe to the place of worship, where the Lord showed that the Judah tribe was guilty. Then Joshua brought the clans of Judah to the Lord, and the Lord showed that the Zerah clan was guilty. One by one he brought the leader of each family in the Zerah clan to the Lord, and the Lord showed that Zabdi's family was guilty.

Joshua 7:7–17 CEV

"I Don't Even Know What to Say to You, God"

Haven't we all been there? Maybe you are there right now, where Joshua was—wordless and filled with one question: Why? I want you to know that is okay. But I also want you to see how God responded to Joshua. My prayer is that you will feel bold enough to say the hard things to God and be brave enough to hear the Spirit say to you, "Stop lying there on the ground. Get up." Joshua had no idea his people hadn't obeyed everything that God told them to do. All Joshua knew was that the children of God were being pummeled by the enemy after a pretty big victory. Joshua's thought process feels so familiar, doesn't it?

Why would you bring us so far only to have us experience defeat after a big victory?

None of this would have happened if we had played it safe and hadn't crossed the Jordan.

This isn't fair.

It wasn't supposed to turn out like this.

Everyone will think you, God, are not strong enough.

Everyone will think that I am not strong enough.

We're gonna die, but first I need to throw a wild-haired fit about it.

This is your turn to throw a fit; I give you permission. Roll around on the floor if you need to. Say the things that you're afraid to say to a God who loves you and gives you space to be human and flawed, yet gloriously His. The work of the Holy Spirit is mutual; it's a team approach, and communication in prayer is vital. Cry those tears if you need to, wrestle it out before the Lord, and then get up, girl! This world and the people in your corner are waiting for you. Get up.

I think it's important to point out that the reason opposition was coming against God's people was because actions have consequences; they had disobeyed the Lord's instructions. They were holding on to items and property that were supposed to be destroyed. Isn't that what we do? We keep things in our lives that aren't God's best for us. At times in my life, I have been aware that the main reason why I wasn't walking in victory was because I had sin in my life that I needed to get rid of and deal with for good. It always starts small but grows into something bigger and more destructive. The lie. The tiny hint of jealousy that has you tearing others down and gossiping to make yourself feel better. The coveting and trying to keep up appearances.

When we go through seasons of unhappiness, our minds begin to wonder if the grass really is greener on the other side of the fence. Ingratitude becomes the bitter root of "If only." *If only my husband paid attention to me like Ann's does to her. If only I were twenty pounds lighter, I would like myself. If only we had more money and less stress, I could be more like Beyoncé.* Our feeling of not being "good enough" morphs into something far more devastating to our joy: "What I have now and what I am experiencing now is never enough." What seems like insecurity can quickly turn into complacency and the grip of perpetual discontentment.

We would all be big, fat liars if we acted like we never sinned. The Bible is clear: We have all fallen short of the glory of God. Not some of us, but all of us. The worst we can do is dress up our sin like the world does and try to make it attractive and acceptable when it's a snare that keeps us from living in a way that leads to the fullness and abundance God has for us.

> For everyone has sinned; we all fall short of God's glorious standard. Yet God, in his grace, freely makes us right in his sight. He did this through Christ Jesus when he freed us from the penalty for our sins.
>
> Romans 3:23–24 NLT

That undeserved kindness from God is our motivation to get rid of the sin in our camp and clean house. Our breakthrough might be a decision to turn away from the sin that is keeping us from becoming who God wants us to be and the women we strive to be. Jesus walked this earth to set hearts free. Not only did He help others unpack their baggage from sin; He removed it. In John chapter 8, the scribes and Pharisees brought to Him a woman caught in the act of adultery. I can't imagine the shame she felt, all eyes on her, with people eager to condemn her and throw stones at her to end her broken life. But not Jesus; He stooped and wrote on the ground as if He did not hear them testing Him. As they hurled accusations at the broken woman with the ginormous baggage, He raised himself up and said: "Let any one of you who is without sin be the first to throw a stone at her" (John 8:7).

And then He writes some more on the ground in a crowd of dirty hearts who need to be confronted with their sin to walk away from the woman who was caught in the act. Where was her so-called lover now, as men called her a whore and picked up large stones to throw at her? One by one they left, and it was just the woman with baggage and Jesus, who mends broken places in ragged hearts, setting them free and removing the stain of sin.

"Where are those accusers of yours? Has no one condemned you?"

"No one, my Lord."

"Neither do I condemn you, go and sin no more."

Pointing to a Promising Future

The more baggage we carry, the more intense our desire is to be loved and to please others. It becomes a craving that is never satisfied and a lingering emptiness that takes us down dusty roads that lead to dead ends in every aspect of our lives. Ragged hearts tend to find people with jagged edges to pierce their tender state, and together they become even more toxic, far more broken than when they first met. For some crazy reason, brokenness attracts brokenness, but when Jesus steps into the picture, brokenness becomes a thing of the past. He is the God who goes out of His way to meet with a broken girl in a broken relationship. Jesus sees the tearstained face and refuses to move on until the stone throwers walk away. He writes in the dirty soil and rewrites this woman's history. Go and sin no more; your slate has been wiped clean.

When the enemy reminds us of our past, let us hold unswervingly to the promise of our future. No matter how many times we fall and fail, we must get back up and remember that moment as Jesus stooped low to write on the ground and set a woman free. That day a woman with a sketchy past met true and lasting love, one that restored hope instead of inflicting shame. Jesus' love is a forever love, not an imitation of it that only wants one thing. We never have to throw ourselves away to earn His love, friend—that's what He did. He laid down His life for you. He made the ultimate sacrifice so we could all live as His beloved, clothed with strength and dignity (Proverbs 31:25). Love walked onto the scene and removed the label of shame, welcoming the woman home baggage-free. I pray we can love like Jesus does when we notice the hurting and the wayward; may we rally around them and help them unpack the baggage they have been carrying around for decades. But before we can do that, we have to take care of our junk. If we can look past all the things we don't understand about the people who live differently than we do, maybe we could be more like Jesus and less judge-y.

We have all sinned and fallen short of the glory of God, and not a single one of us has it all together no matter how long we have been serving Christ (Romans 3:23). Let us be grace givers, not stone throwers, for this is the heartbeat of Christ to seek and to save those who are lost (Luke 19:10). I pray I never forget the way I came to Christ and my all-consuming need for a Savior. The Jesus who writes in the dirty soil is unafraid of a dirty past, wiping the slate clean and rewriting our story where baggage becomes a platform, under our feet—exactly where it should be. Sister, you are clean. If you asked Jesus to forgive you, maybe it's time for you to forgive yourself, too. What this woman needed to hear from Jesus more than anything was, "I did not come to condemn you, I came to free you. You don't have to carry around your baggage from shame; no stones hurled in your direction, just love and a fresh start. Walk in that, daughter of God."

Truth Your Soul Needs

I want you to picture something powerful. Imagine each stone of accusation that others tried to throw in your direction falling down at your feet. Now imagine yourself not picking up those stones and collecting them. Imagine yourself walking away set free and loved, with your head held high.

This is our declaration of faith for our breakthrough journey:

If God's Word is true, His Word is true for me.
If His promises are real, then His promises belong to me and are for me.
If His grace is real, His grace covers me.
If He is a God who rescues, He is a God who rescues me.
If He is a God who heals, He wants to heal and mend me.

Reflective Questions

1. What stolen property do you need to reclaim from the enemy?
2. Do you seek sturdy confidence over insecurity? Faith to quiet your loudest fears?

3. Do you need boldness that is bigger than timidity and a ginormous inferiority complex? Security in who God made you to be over identity issues and self-doubt?

Gutsy Prayer

Often the enemy tries to distract us when we are hurting. Our focus is naturally on what hurts and what is causing us pain. One way to place the focus back on God is through praise. And we can praise Him in our prayers. When we worship and thank God for who He is and what He has done and will do for us, we experience a calm well beyond any chaos and an undeniable peace through a changed perspective.

Lord,

I praise you, for you are a sun and a shield around me. You lavish me with grace and withhold no good thing from me as I purpose in my heart to walk upright before you (Psalm 84:11).

Amen.

5

Questions Jesus Asked and Why We Still Need to Ask Them

When Jesus interacted with people, it was the beginning of their breakthrough, and each breakthrough led them to an action they needed to take. Like go and sin no more, take up your mat and walk. Breakthrough is not the end or even the resolution; it is a transition to go deeper into your relationship with Christ and your faith. Jesus moved them beyond their need by asking them questions.

When my daughters tell me something hurts, I don't want to just know that it hurts; I want them to get specific and show me. To spell it out, point to the problem, and give me something that I can work with so I can do my best to help. If there is something I can do, I will move heaven and earth to do it. And, as fierce and intense as my love is for my girls, it doesn't even come close to how much God loves us. It's almost too much to wrap our minds around, but it's true.

There is something so powerful about verbalizing our needs to God because it forces us to acknowledge our needs instead of pretending there isn't pain or a real problem in our life. If our relationship with our Savior resembled the close relationships we have with others in our lives, would we hold back, pretending all was well when everything in our world was frayed at the seams and coming undone?

"What do you want me to do for you?"

Matthew 20:32

It seems pretty simple, doesn't it? It feels like this should fall into the category of easy-peasy, telling Jesus what we need from Him or crying out to Him in prayer, but often enough we paint Jesus into the same place as the people who disappointed us and left us stranded when we were at our lowest point. But Jesus is bigger. Jesus reaches further. And Jesus never runs out on us when the weight of the world is stacked against us. And still, we paint Him in human colors and limit Him. But we serve a limitless God unchained by our misunderstandings of His power.

Jesus came wrapped in flesh and understood the limitations of our humanity yet remained who He is, the perfect Son of God who came to take away our sins. He is not the man who wanted more than you could give and threw you away the minute you stood up for yourself. God is not the voice in your head shaming you, saying you are not enough. God is telling you that *He* is enough. That He is the great I AM. Who He is inside of you is more than enough to take care of whatever you are facing today or what you will face in the future.

Jesus is not tired of you. Jesus is waiting and unafraid of your questions. Maybe your daddy is gone like mine is, and perhaps you have a heart-daddy like I have, a stepdad who stepped in and has loved you as flesh and blood. Maybe your picture of the Father's love is hazy, like an impressionistic painting where the lines of what is real and what is false are blurred and unable to be fully grasped. My prayer for you today is that you will see Jesus in a way that causes you to relax and trust Him even when nothing makes sense to you.

Let's peel back some layers and go straight to the heart of Jesus in the pages of the Bible, shall we?

As I began studying the questions Jesus asked in the Bible and why it's essential for us to ask ourselves (and answer) those questions today, I knew I needed to begin by asking a question I believe will help you find answers and healing in a way that will be solid and life-changing. One question Jesus asked His disciples was, "Who do people say that I am?"

The disciples gave their answer. The people thought Jesus could have been anyone other than who He was. Some confused Him with John the Baptist, Jeremiah, Elijah, and some of the other prophets. But Jesus' question was a leading one; something far more significant was about to be asked of them. "But who do you say I am?" It didn't matter who others thought Jesus was. It didn't matter what the crowd mentality was back then, or even what the crowd mentality is right now in this jacked-up world. The crowd believed Him to be anyone other than their Savior and their redemption. Even now, the world wants a nicer, watered-down Jesus who turns a blind eye to sins—a do-whatever-makes-you-happy Jesus. But, my Jesus is a chain breaker, not a pushover. His boundaries are our blessings, not a buzzkill.

> When Jesus came into the region of Caesarea Philippi, He asked His disciples, saying, "Who do men say that I, the Son

> of Man, am?" So they said, "Some say John the Baptist, some Elijah, and others Jeremiah or one of the prophets." He said to them, "But who do you say that I am?" Simon Peter answered and said, "You are the Christ, the Son of the living God." Jesus answered and said to him, "Blessed are you, Simon Bar-Jonah, for flesh and blood has not revealed this to you, but My Father who is in heaven. And I also say to you that you are Peter, and on this rock I will build My church, and the gates of Hades shall not prevail against it. And I will give you the keys of the kingdom of heaven, and whatever you bind on earth will be bound in heaven, and whatever you loose on earth will be loosed in heaven."
>
> Matthew 16:13–19 NKJV

Who Do You Say Jesus Is?

If your answer, even in your heartache and confusion, is *He is the Christ*, your response alone will help you make sense of what you feel versus what you believe and line it up with the truth. Maybe we can't know who we are as women until we know exactly who Jesus is. Jesus is life abundantly and freedom to the fullest. Jesus is the friend of the outcasts and those misunderstood by many. Jesus is the guy people wanted at their parties. Jesus is the one who felt moved in His gut when He saw the pressing needs of His people.

Jesus saw something extraordinary in ordinary people and called them to leave everything that made sense and the only life they had known to follow Him. Peter, in all of his flawed humanity, became a rock Christ could build his church on, and isn't that exactly what Jesus wants for all of us? I believe it is. Your sinking doubts, the way you wrestle—wondering if you are a lost cause and even worth God's time—can vanish by asking yourself one of the most important questions you will ever answer: Who do you say Jesus is?

If you believe Jesus is your answer, solution, and the air you breathe, then eventually, perhaps sooner rather than later, you will know exactly how God sees you. If we believe Jesus is real, then we will trust He will be real and powerfully present in our pain. When our answer is delayed for the hundredth time, and the pain is unbearable, and even when all hell is breaking loose, we can live unshaken because of the power of Christ in us. We are a rock, not a dishrag. We are powerful, not powerless. When we stand in Jesus' strength, we stand ready and more than able to handle the hard things in life. This world does not need our watered-down Jesus. It is desperate for the real Jesus—the one who goes out of the way for the wayward.

Maybe today you feel like an outcast in cute shoes wearing a plastic smile, and perhaps you have spent much of your life trying to keep up with everyone else, convinced that you are farther away from Jesus and not only questioning your identity, but His, as well. Rewind, start fresh today and build from this place. Rock bottom is the perfect place to begin again, building your life on the truth in God's Word.

"Do You Believe I Am Able to Do This for You?"

Two blind men couldn't see the man named Jesus the whole town was talking about, but they had heard about the miracle-worker. They wanted to experience the miracle and mystery of Jesus, desperate for opened eyes that could see. I love how Jesus cuts to the chase. My Southern-girl hospitality often drives me to dance around the issues and play nice. "Do you believe I am able to do this for you?" A two-word answer from two blind men was all it took for healing to take place. "Yes, Lord." Then

Jesus spoke one sentence that caused blind eyes to see, their cloudy eyes no match for the faith in their souls: "According to your faith let it be done to you" (Matthew 9:29).

For a minute or two after I read these words in this familiar passage, I waited for those powerful words to sink into the soul of this faith-filled woman. I'm aware of how many times my level of faith doesn't even scratch the surface of what my all-powerful God can do. At times we have a watered-down faith when we serve a water-walking Jesus. He doesn't just walk on water; He let fumbling Peter walk on water, too, even if it was only for a minute. According to his faith level, Peter sank. Aren't we just like two-second Peter? We are sinking when Jesus made it possible for us to stand. *Jesus, help us to run on water and do the impossible things with a tenacious faith that says, "Yes, Lord. My faith is bigger than everything this world might try to throw at me."*

Do you believe Jesus is able?

Are you ready to live like you believe it?

Are you ready for your eyes to be opened?

Are you ready to walk in faith like never before?

Do you want to be well?

Traveling Light

It was a sticky-hot summer day, and I found myself wanting to connect with women who are part of my online tribe. I wanted to ask questions and get a feel for what they were facing and experiencing in life. When one sweet lady commented, tears filled my eyes because I understood what she was feeling.

"I want to know what traveling light looks like. I want to know how to truly lay some heavy stuff down."

Sweet friend, this is the exact question I had asked myself for years, so I knew I had to respond in the purest state of emotional buck-nakedness. And I'm okay with that. Tomorrow I will drive home, sign some papers, and say one more painful good-bye as my sister and I close on my father's automotive and upholstery shop. At one time, it was the picture of a passionate perfectionist who took pride in the way things looked and a job well done. But now it's just a run-down shop that holds so many good memories, yet so many brutal ones, as well. But mostly, it's a mess that I see so much potential in, and apparently, the new owners do, too. The ache I feel isn't because I'm bitter. I ache because I am still laying down some heavy stuff, but I'm not walking away empty-handed. I'm walking away openhearted and most likely holding my baby sister's hand.

I can point to the place where they found my father. I can tell you where I was standing when I realized that addiction had taken over and left his shell. I couldn't see it then, but I do now. It was pain. It was a bad heart and a bent back. It was a few pills and a bottle when what he needed was surgery. But which one do you fix first when you're that broken? In the end, his pain became more than he could bear. As his health declined, everything else in his life followed suit. Once again, I lay down those hard things to cling to the good memories of when he was fully present in our lives. I'll whisper about the sweet and happy memories when the ugly ones are loud and haunting.

Tomorrow I will hand over the keys and remind myself that I'm a grown woman because saying good-bye to that shop means saying good-bye once again to my dad and the little brown-eyed girl inside of me. I'm going to tell her that she did it. She became everything she dreamed she could be. She's soft yet strong. I'll tell her that she's whole and better than okay. I'll tell her that when she learned to love big and forgive quickly and often until it stuck, that pattern kept her load light and her heart free. I'll tell her that Jesus was bigger than everything that tried (and failed) to break her.

I have learned how to travel light because I have learned the repetitive motion of forgiveness: You continue to forgive and release the hurts until it no longer stings. Finally, you get to move on with a lighter load and battle scars that fade. You trade the victim labels for a better identity that brave girls like you truly deserve. I have learned to travel light because I have learned not to carry things that don't belong to me. That's super hard for us because we are mat carriers and fixers.

In John 5:6–8, Jesus noticed a man who had been an invalid for thirty-eight years.

Jesus asked the beggar a very important question: "Do you want to be well?" After thirty-eight years, you would think it would be a quick "yes!" But, at some point, the man had stopped trying.

> Some time later, Jesus went up to Jerusalem for one of the Jewish festivals. Now there is in Jerusalem near the Sheep Gate a pool, which in Aramaic is called Bethesda and which is surrounded by five covered colonnades. Here a great number of disabled people used to lie—the blind, the lame, the paralyzed. One who was there had been an invalid for thirty-eight years. When Jesus saw him lying there and learned that he had been in this condition for a long time, he asked him, "Do you want to get well?"
>
> "Sir," the invalid replied, "I have no one to help me into the pool when the water is stirred. While I am trying to get in, someone else goes down ahead of me."
>
> Then Jesus said to him, "Get up! Pick up your mat and walk." At once the man was cured; he picked up his mat and walked.
>
> John 5:1–9

When Jesus asked him if he wanted to be well, his reply was, "I have no one to help me into the pool." His "Pick up your mat and walk" moment reminds me that it's never too late to find the healing our soul or body needs. It also reminds me that often we find it easier to blame someone else for what's wrong with us—the wounds we feel justified in carrying around like a mat we no longer need.

The loss of my father still hurts; I still feel a little sad, and that's okay. I can still grieve while giving myself room to feel everything without picking up the mat of regret and if-only. My breakthrough happened because I wanted to be well and free from my past, and I was willing to wrestle it out and find God in the breaking. I learned how to let go and realized that I couldn't carry the mat of everyone else in my life and stay sane.

The invalid's healing required action on his part. He had to want it, pick up his mat, and leave the place where he had dwelled for so long. I imagine that he didn't want to keep his mat just in case he needed it later. I bet he trashed it. Or made table mats out of it because the place he used to be stuck was the very place where Jesus met him and provided for him.

You can travel light. You can lay your mat down because you don't need it anymore. You can face hard things and ache with a hopeful heart that understands God will always meet you in your place of pain. But He doesn't force-feed us or carry our mats for us. We are an active participant in our healing. Trust. Obey. Forgive. Repeat. You can do this. Don't settle for anything less than a lighter load.

Truth Your Soul Needs

Our human nature causes us to revert to our old ways. Why do we go back to the things that cripple us? Because, like the beggar, we become comfortable with crutches, mats, and placing blame. Jesus asked specific questions of the people who were in need. This reminds me that God wants us to be very specific in naming what we need freedom or healing from. This is how we bring our pain to Jesus and invite the light.

Isn't it time to break up with your invisible crutch?

Reflective Question

What are the things—or who are the people—you have been leaning on instead of trusting Jesus?

Gutsy Prayer

I know listing your personal crutches wasn't easy to do. But you did it. Let's seal this moment with a prayer to help you with what you are feeling right now and keep you moving forward!

Lord,

I come to you ready to lay down my mat and the crutches that I have leaned on. I ask for your help and guidance to move forward in my life by realizing that those things I have clung to have actually kept me from you, not empowered me. I know that you are mighty and able to take care of everything that concerns me (Psalm 138:8). I recognize that my need to control and do things on my own has crippled me.

I am ready to walk in the freedom you have for me. I believe this will become my norm, walking in your power and freedom daily. I lay down my pride. I throw off my weights of doubt and fear to run the race you have called me to (Hebrews 12:1). I praise you for the way you have given me the ability to hear your voice.

I praise you for the weapon of your Word and ask for your courage to wield the sword and root up strongholds in my life. Your Word is alive and active inside of me; sharper than any double-edged sword, it penetrates even to dividing soul and spirit, joints and marrow, and judges the thoughts and attitudes of my heart (Hebrews 4:12). Thank you for loving me and setting me free today and always.

In Jesus' name, amen.

6

Freedom from Your Inner Mean Girl

When I walked into my first rehearsal for Miss Small Town USA, with a sack containing two greasy corndogs and large fries in one hand and a gallon-sized soda in the other, I knew I might be in the wrong place. Some of those girls hadn't eaten in weeks, and just the smell of my lunch made most of them want to vomit. But I was about to walk my first figure-8 in a swimsuit and four-inch nude heels; I needed fuel! When I looked around the room, everything inside of me felt out of place. I had just a few days to figure out how to get a fake tan and boobs to fill up my swimsuit. I wanted to die the death of a flat-chested girl with big hair.

One girl politely handed me two squishy things that looked like chicken cutlets, and she told me the best way to hoist those babies up was good old-fashioned duct tape. Let me say now *not* to do this. Like, ever. In a bathroom filled with girls who had no problem showing their junk, my chicken cutlets were taped up and in place—with silver duct tape. Classy or trashy?

You decide. It took only two pageant girls to make the cleavage magic happen while I stood there feeling slightly thankful that they had only mildly violated me. Later, when I ripped off the duct tape, I said a string of words that would make a drunken sailor blush. I uttered all the words that I had gasped at when I heard them spoken in the past by the kids who spent a lot of time in juvie and started smoking in middle school. I would never say words like that—I swore on my pink NIV Bible—but when you rip off three layers of skin on the count of three, a girl has to swear a little. I asked Jesus to forgive me and then promised to never duct tape my underdeveloped boobs again.

I might have looked pretty and polished with everything in place (thank you, duct tape and Aqua Net), but I didn't feel like I fit at all. I learned so many things about myself through those experiences, but the lesson that followed me through dress fittings and two hours of hair and makeup was that I didn't want to be fake. I was fine with the big hair and learning how to walk in four-inch heels, but I refused to be something I wasn't—a girl who looked and acted like everyone else. I could be poised standing on a stage, but I was anything but polished and was in full-on dork mode moments later when I removed the chicken cutlets and drag-queen makeup. How could I learn to love and accept all of me, not to mention the less-developed parts? If I could go back and talk to my younger self, I would tell her that this would take a while, and to stay away from pageant girls with silver tape who smile too much.

> If our perfect Lord is gracious enough to take our worst, and ugliest, our most boring, our least successful, and forgive them, burying them in the depths of the sea, then it's high time we give each other a break.
>
> Charles Swindoll[1]

I have unpacked a mother lode of baggage in the spotlight of ministry and have learned something profound about dealing with insecurity and filtering out the voice of critics. Not every voice—especially if it's a negative one—deserves to be heard. We want to listen to the right voices, the ones that inspire us and motivate us. I am all for constructive criticism and listening to wise and godly counsel. We can learn from everything, whether it's said in love or not, but sometimes it would be nice if we could have a mute button for people—including ourselves.

Of all the negative words and the not-so-nice things that have been said to me, none of the harm can even compare with the damage done by the hateful girl who used to live in my head. Her venom made the other girls' voices seem like grade school taunting that barely even caused a sting or purplish-yellow bruises. I have learned to let those hard words go; they roll off like rain on a tin roof. I do not collect them or rehearse old conversations turned sour. Keeping records of wrongs does absolutely nothing for your well-being, trust me on this. But before I could release things and forgive those hurtful words from the past or even present, I first had to learn how to be kind to myself.

I am what I call a sloppy perfectionist with tendencies of OCD and ADD, so everything has to be perfect. But with an attention span like mine, perfection never lasts very long. True story. So beating myself up is easy to do on the regular because I am a total spaz. But that silliness is something I have come to enjoy about myself as someone with a profound need for spontaneity. Life is so much sweeter when you learn how to enjoy it instead of taking yourself so seriously. There has to be room in our lives for slip-ups and mistakes. You are going to forget something, run late at times, and say something you wished you hadn't, because we are flawed people. There will be a long list of mistakes from now until we take our final breath, but we do not have to collect an equally long list of regrets if we extend kindness and grace to others and ourselves.

Inner Mean Girls' Words Are Not God's

I have worked closely with women of all ages for twenty years and have had countless conversations on the topic of how mean we are to ourselves. This morning when I sat down to write, tears came on your behalf so quickly, along with an ache in my heart because of the inner battle you probably wage against yourself on a daily basis. You are the treasure of God's heart. You are not just one of His children; you're a chosen one, and vastly wanted, and worth the big deal I am making over you. I would gush more if I thought you would keep reading.

After all of the warm, fuzzy feelings left me, I became increasingly ticked off when talking to a few good women about the ugly talk going on in their heads. It became even more apparent that our most significant breakthrough and battle starts and ends in our mind. Hers is the voice no one else can hear, but she taunts you relentlessly and tells you that you'll never be good enough. I'm not sure when she took up residence in your pretty head, but I need to talk with her. I need you to see how stark the contrast is between what she has led you to believe and what God says and thinks about you. You can't have a breakthrough until you have a come-to-Jesus meeting with the mean girl in your head. I'm ready to pick a fight with her. I am 110 percent sure that if we team up and go to war with God on our side, we are going to win this battle. She has to go. Replace her voice with one you can live with, and begin to thrive in the abundant life God has for you. It's time for her to be on your side.

You are your worst critic. Even on good days, when the mean girl knows you are crushing it, she's still sizing you up and telling you a million things you could have done better. She says one hundred hateful things every day: You could look better, could have said that differently, handled that hard situation better. That voice is not your better self trying to get out. It's the reason you feel like you never measure up, and how could you when perfection wouldn't even make your inner mean girl happy? The list is long and cruel: You could have done your presentation without faltering, parented without losing your cool, and put more effort into something not even worth your time. But you couldn't outrun the voice in your head talking down to you. How could you when you've welcomed her voice and allowed her too much room instead of showing her the door? Don't you think it's time to hush her and teach her how to play nice?

> Wholehearted living is about engaging in our lives from a place of worthiness. It means cultivating the courage, compassion, and connection to wake up in the morning and think, *No matter what gets done and how much is left undone, I am enough.* It's going to bed at night thinking, *Yes, I am imperfect and vulnerable and sometimes afraid, but that doesn't change the truth that I am also brave and worthy of love and belonging.*
>
> Brené Brown[2]

I asked a question of my tribe on social media: What does your inner voice sound like? Is she negative or positive? Who does she sound like? I can honestly say I wasn't surprised by the answers, but even so, I found my heart breaking again for the lies godly women like you believe. A majority of the women confessed that their inner voice was mostly negative; some even threw in a percentage because they know how much room she has taken up with mean talk. One woman replied, "My inner voice sounds like a bunch of Sunday school teachers reminding me that I don't measure up." Note: If this is what your Sunday school teachers sound like, you need to find a new class.

I found myself wondering who planted those seeds of negativity within you. Maybe it was a person in authority over you or a bully at school, or perhaps it was someone in your family with a critical eye and a loose tongue so eager to say whatever entered their mind—but only if it was unkind and ugly. Seeds are planted by others who have spoken hurtful things to us, but only we can water and feed those thoughts. We alone hold the power over them, and that's why it's up to us to dig up those deeply rooted insecurities and replace them with the truth. We cannot fight lies with lies; we fight them with the truth.

One of my favorite passages, found in 2 Corinthians 10:5, is about taking every thought captive to obey Christ, and I found a translation that calls out the issue at heart:

> We destroy arguments and every lofty opinion raised against the knowledge of God, and take every thought captive to obey Christ.
>
> 2 Corinthians 10:5 ESV

We are made in the likeness of God, designed by Him and for Him. Not some of us, but all of us. When we bash who we are, we are bashing God's handiwork and calling it not enough instead of fearfully and wonderfully made (Psalm 139). I wonder what would happen if we would go so far to say that our inner mean girl isn't just talking trash, but she is disobedient to God's design and plan for you? That God's heart is so for you that anything that doesn't line up with His love for you must come into alignment with His ultimate plan for you. It's time for all of us as women and believers to get on board with God's heart for us, to have a holy reverence to receive all the love, grace, and forgiveness He paid for with humility, to welcome it with an eager heart.

We are all undeserving, but that didn't stop the most beautiful sacrifice anyone could give on our behalf. He whom the Son has set free is free indeed (John 8:36). She is free. She is wanted. Her sins have been paid for, so she doesn't have to beat herself up anymore. She doesn't have to hustle for her worth or jump through a million hoops, hoping to receive love based on her performance. She is wholeheartedly loved beyond measure. She is God's delight. Many women do excellent and noble things, but she surpasses them all (Proverbs 31:29). The people in her corner think she's pretty great because she radiates the glory of God and serves the ones around her well. That, my friend, is who you are. Get on board with that and walk into every room knowing that nothing you do or say can change the love God has for you. You don't have to measure up to be filled to overflowing with the abundance God has for you. Jesus Christ has already paid your debt, dear one. It's time for you to open your heart (all the way this time) and receive it.

Heart-to-Heart Talk

Take a few minutes to write down five things that you like about yourself. Yes, five.

Now write out a prayer asking God to help you use those five things to honor Him. Take time to thank Him for the gifts He has given you, and ask for new eyes to see yourself as God sees you.

Revelation and knowledge of who we are in Christ becomes the gift that keeps on giving. Write down the name of one woman who struggles with this and beats herself up on a daily basis. Will you take a few minutes not only to pray for her but also to send her a card or message to encourage her heart? Let's storm enemy territory and love someone the way we so desperately have needed it in the past!

> Let's be gentle with each other and ourselves, tender toward our failures.
>
> It can be an act of worship to remember we are only human, not GOD after all.
>
> Holley Gerth[3]

Sometimes I think we are tall toddlers learning how to talk and play nicely with the woman we look at in the mirror; we have wasted so much time tearing her down and telling her she's not enough. The running dialogue in our heads is a powerful one. I think it's more than okay to call out that voice and ask it some questions: "Do you line up with God's truth?" If the answer is, "Meh, maybe God hates me, too?" then we have work to do. But if the honest answer is, "I'm working on it," it's time to prove that with what we allow to occupy our brain and heart space. Let's arm ourselves with better tools.

What does freedom look like, and how can we flourish, even on the bad days? Grace. Grace. And more grace.

> But he said to me, "My grace is sufficient for you, for my power is made perfect in weakness." Therefore I will boast all the more gladly about my weaknesses, so that Christ's power may rest on me.
>
> 2 Corinthians 12:9

Be Nice

> "If you can't say something nice about yourself, practice."
>
> —Unknown

I heard someone say that our inner voice sounds a lot like our mother's. Frankly, as a mother of teenage daughters, that scares me senseless. If that is true, what will the voice in my daughter's head sound like twenty years from now? There is no way to be sure, but it if helps them to brush their teeth and not run around in their underwear all day, I'll consider it mostly positive. I'm the voice telling both of them they can do all things through Christ. Not just some things, or a few things that aren't that important, but everything they set their hearts and minds to do. On stressful days I'm like the voice of a broken record, saying the same things over and over until I'm frustrated, and then the volume gets cranked up.

It's in the meaningful conversations with my girls when they become painfully honest; I feel the pain in my heart with the realization that the voices in their heads sound a lot like mine does in moments of weakness. It seems like preplanned defeat and crippling fear telling them to stay safe and small. It echoes like taunting and shame-slinging, reminding them that no matter what, they will somehow fall short. But that's where the mama bear comes in as I tell them to shut those voices down and send them back to where they came from. I lean in close and tell them all the reasons those voices are lies that they have to uproot and replace with truth, and how I have to do the same thing. And I will keep doing this until one day it becomes the truest voice in their head.

Any voice that does not line up with the Word of God has to leave. Any voice that is condemning and puts a barrier between you and finding Jesus to be your source and ultimate companion who lovingly corrects you has to be dealt with—like the voice of shame that says, "You can stop trying now because you'll never be worthy enough." We all have those thoughts surface, and most of us know exactly when they began. Unfortunately, those voices begin much too soon in the hearts of God's children, and whether or not those voices sound a lot like someone who had influence over us or raised us, it's not up to anyone but us to quiet them and banish them from taking up sacred space in our hearts. Beautiful one, how you talk to yourself is powerful. If I could sit across from you right now, I would take your hand in mine and be your overprotective sister, asking you one question: "Is the voice in your head nice to you, or does that voice make you feel tired and like a failure?"

How will we ever win our battles if we don't recognize that our power begins in our minds?

It took years for the voice in our head to develop, but with the power of God dwelling within, we can take back enemy territory and gain ground by speaking truth over our hearts. All it takes is one determined woman ready to not only have her breakthrough, but to fight for it. We wage war the right way; we pace the floor in prayer or curl up in our prayer closet with tears streaming down our face. We can yell and shake our fist at the devil, and we can be certain that we are powerful because we have the power of Christ inside of us. We are the weak becoming strong. Okay, so you are struggling in this area; let's fix that together with a plan. Here's a battle plan for making your inner mean girl toe the line.

The Word is your personal weapon.

Study key Scriptures and write them down, putting them in a place where you will look at them every day. Here are a few Scriptures to start with.

> He is your constant source of stability;
> he abundantly provides safety and great wisdom;
> he gives all this to those who fear him.
>
> Isaiah 33:6 NET

> For God hath not given us a spirit of fear; but of power, and of love, and of a sound mind.
>
> 2 Timothy 1:7 KJV

> Stand firm then, with the belt of truth buckled around your waist, with the breastplate of righteousness in place, and with your feet fitted with the readiness that comes from the gospel of peace. In addition to all this, take up the shield of faith, with which you can extinguish all the flaming arrows of the evil one. Take the helmet of salvation and the sword of the Spirit, which is the word of God.
>
> Ephesians 6:14–17

Woman to woman: Have an accountability partner or mentor.

Finding a guide or mentor doesn't have to be daunting. I know it's easier said than done to find a mentor or friend to walk alongside you, but I encourage you to start by extending an invitation for coffee or lunch and go from there. Go to a Bible study with other women, find someone further along in their faith journey than you are, and get to know her. Ask her if you can have tea or coffee with her and tell her you would like her insight on how to grow in this area. Side note: Don't dump everything on her on a first friend date. Get to know her and let her get to know you! What I have learned from talking with many older women is that they have felt rejected in the past by younger women, or have felt like they have overstepped boundaries. By reaching out to her first, you make this easier on her.

Just in Case You Didn't Know, People Can Be Mean

When Paul talked about his thorn in the flesh in 2 Corinthians 12, he spoke honestly about how he prayed and asked God to remove it. And while many think it likely that Paul was referring to a physical limitation, when I hear people talking about their "thorn in the flesh," most of the time they are referring to someone who gets under their skin and makes them want to swear a little. Oh, honey, I am in ministry and relate to this line of thinking because I have personally experienced those rare few people who nobody but Jesus himself could please. I also know how hard it is to lead those who are determined not to like anything you do or say. And maybe we become too caught up with naming the person who gives us the most grief in our lives. But most of the time, the thorn in our flesh is the fact that we are flawed flesh and blood. It's easier to place blame than it is to stomach the knowledge that we are the most significant thing standing in our way.

Freedom is about releasing those things we tend to find satisfaction in to own our part in the blame game, to not sit in our shame but to reach out to the God who formed us and made us for more than second best. God's best for us doesn't include withholding blessings from us. His best for us often requires a healthy amount of grit and tears to make it through each obstacle laid out before us. God didn't call you to be a thorn or to cower to the thorns in your life. He called you to thrive even when life is hard. We get to choose what we allow to be the thorns in our lives.

My thorn is seasonal depression and anxiety. Even though I am on a low dose of medication to help me manage it, I still have plenty of anxiety to spare and the wit about me to fight by faith when life threatens to dampen my spark. Several years ago, I had swirling shreds of memories and used Kleenexes in my lap as I sat in a counselor's office. It was wintertime and I felt myself sinking again. Some call it seasonal depression. Some call it lingering sadness. Either way, it's pretty brutal.

I'm an overachiever when it comes to dealing with my junk, so I took out my prayer journal on those nights of endless wrestling with my thoughts and sheet covers. I had figured out the root of my depression. It was only four words, but those four words took me down toxic trails that caused me to try harder and to spend myself to the point of exhaustion. I was just the human version of a show dog jumping through hoops. The words rolled out, and clarity came. Those four words took on a much larger shape of unrealistic expectations.

Those four words became a foundation that I built upon, walls and rooms filled with striving and measuring sticks. The devil is a punk, using the same tricks on all of us. It's the same four words on repeat: "I am not enough." Later, those four words became, "I am not okay."

For every lie we believe, there is a stronger, more powerful truth found in God's Word. I started praying Scriptures. Sometimes I could only pray one-word prayers like "Help." But, I knew that was enough because I learned the power of a God who specializes in wordless groans. The Spirit helps us in our weakness. When we don't know what to pray for, the Spirit himself intercedes for us through those wordless groans (Romans 8:26). God has us covered so we don't have to worry about having the right words to pray. I learned how to take thoughts captive and figured out that it was possible for me to be the boss of my emotions instead of my emotions bossing me. (For example: I'm not a good wife . . . daughter . . . friend. . . . I don't call enough . . . do enough . . . reach out enough . . . cook enough . . . workout enough . . .) When those feelings surface and try to take the shape of those four very small words that used to feel like the biggest punch in the face, I shut it all the way down.

Freedom from our Not-Enough List is calling those feelings out. What are your areas of not enough?

___

___

___

___

God Is More than Enough

If real love is unconditional, why on earth are we working so hard to earn it? I believe it comes from a sweet and sincere place of wanting to love and be loved, but people-pleasing is our Kryptonite. Do we want to be everything for our family and friends? Yes. But can we? Girl, you are not Jesus. He is alive and active inside of you, but you still only have twenty-four hours in your day just like everyone else does. We cannot be all things to all people. If we recognize that our love for others is fierce, loyal, and grace-giving, we can trust that our people can love us back like that. Will we still try hard? Of course we will. But this time we can know that we are enough even when we are not, even when we feel like we are too much and talk too much or say too little.

When we are weak, God is more than enough. He is the foundation we need that is filled with provision and grace. When you let Him inside your heart and let Him have access to every facet of who you are, you will not find one room where shame is free to live. There are treasures hidden in dark places, and sometimes we have to mine for the diamonds in the stark, cold night. We have to dig into His Word and go to counseling and do the hard work to be free.

> And I will give you treasures hidden in the darkness—secret riches. I will do this so you may know that I am the Lord, the God of Israel, the one who calls you by name.
>
> Isaiah 45:3 NLT

Scriptures to pray through until you get your breakthrough.

> Casting down arguments and every high thing that exalts itself against the knowledge of God, bringing every thought into captivity to the obedience of Christ . . .
>
> 2 Corinthians 10:5 NKJV

> In the same way, the Spirit helps us in our weakness. We do not know what we ought to pray for, but the Spirit himself intercedes for us through wordless groans.
>
> Romans 8:26

Shame Doesn't Live Here Anymore

After years and years fighting on my own, a little voice in my head said, "Are you done?" Are you done shaming and shoulding all over the place? Are you done with feeling small and ashamed of your thorn? Do you know that you are worth seeking treatment and getting the help you need? Are you ready to be whole?

My answer was yes. It was time for me to explore medical treatment. Everyone has a different journey, and mine includes trying and managing on my own for way longer than I probably should have, and then seeking help from a medical professional. After wrestling for years, I made an appointment with my doctor. I was fresh out of tears; I was too tired and battle weary, but I was determined to be gutsy enough to do whatever it took to feel awake again. I checked off all of my boxes in the counselor's office. I worked through every area of personal baggage, and this girl knew her soul was as free as it could be.

I walked out of that doctor's office with my head held high and hope in my heart. The next morning I took my first antidepressant, and I didn't chase it down with shame. I chased it down with Coca-Cola Classic and hope that reminded me that while I still felt unwell and weak, my worth and strength of will was more powerful than ever. I waited, prayed, and like clockwork every morning I took a tiny little pill and clung to hope that my thorn would no longer be at the forefront of my mind. After a few months went by, the real Jennifer surfaced, and I genuinely liked that awake version of the girl I knew when I was younger. I was back, and it was—and still is—glorious.

"Don't Give Breath to That"

If you only knew how long it took for me to realize that being angry wasn't sinning. It is what we do with the anger that crosses us over from being furiously peeved to hell-has-no-fury. I wonder if British playwright William Congreve knew when he penned *The Mourning Bride* in 1697 that it would live on forever in the hearts of men and become so much more of a warning than two short lines: "Heav'n has no rage like love to hatred turn'd. Nor Hell a fury, like a woman scorn'd."[4] Who knew this would become popular in movies and books, and quoted by all? While it's funny to think about, any person who has felt the sting of an angry woman knows it's not funny at all; it's downright terrifying.

I'm one of those annoying people who rarely get mad. But when I do, girl, hold my earrings. In my twenties, I really didn't know what I was angry about, so my approach was to start rattling off everything my young, wide-eyed husband had done in the last few weeks, maybe even years, and eventually I would find the root of why I was upset. The hard thing about this was that Jonathan's mind was spinning with the first angry word spoken, and he was already placed on the defensive by phrases such as *you always* and *you never* before I got to the real issue.

When you settle into who you are and walk in freedom, your emotions are less roller-coaster-like and unstable. Now I can form an intelligent sentence and get straight to the heart of the issue. Does it still put my man on the defensive? At times, yes. Do I still use the wrong words that feel unfair to him at times? Of course I do. We are two very different people trying to be one flesh when everything inside of us tells us we are two distinct entities who need different things to function and be somewhat happy. But my life looked differently then than it does now. When I was working through a few things in my life that were unhealed, I had specific triggers that I had to work harder to get over. We all have them, and I bet most of them are similar. One of mine was tied to rejection and feeling unaccepted at the beginning of my relationship with my husband, when we first started dating and I was wondering if we were more than just friends.

I can happily say that heartache faded into the background, because two polar opposites decided that our love and relationship was worth the risky disapproval of friends and family. And that we were capable of hearing from God. Despite the talk of how wrong we were for each other, we fell in love, disregarding the better judgment of others. I was so eager to please back then and wanted not only to be liked—I wanted to be loved and accepted. My disease to please caused me to twist inside and jump through hoops, hoping that if I was good enough, I would prove my worth. No one put that pressure on me; I was to blame. I was the willing party inflicting so much pain because I couldn't get over that at first I was a question mark. But in the eyes of that crazy tall guy falling in love with me, it wasn't a question mark. I was his biggest exclamation point, and that should have been enough for me. But it wasn't, because of my insecurities. For every taunting lie saying we are not good enough, we shout it louder, "The way I feel now, God, isn't enough for me, either!"

One evening as I vented to a mothering mentor, I went deeper into the why behind my frustration and disconnect with my loved ones. But it went past the lines of confession to heal and let go, to validation and finger-pointing. Frankly, I was ticked, and it was ugly. As I began to relive and rehash moments in an unhealthy way, my mentor said, "Don't give breath to that." She meant that my words were only stirring up toxic thoughts and reopening old wounds, which was the exact reason I was stuck emotionally. There was a battle going on in my heart, and I had the power to stop it.

We all have our stories and battle scars, and I would never tell you that your scars aren't stories worth being retold and worth fresh tears. I will never minimize your pain. Never. But because I love you, I must tell you some truth. We will always be wasting our breath when we are stirring up toxic thoughts and slinging blame in every direction. We are not being strong in those moments of spewing our negativity to whoever will listen. We are made smaller and powerless as we open the door to the enemy. He delights in twisting our stories and painting them a darker shade of hopeless.

We do not have to minimize our pain, not ever, but when we magnify our God, the power goes to the healer and mender of our stories. Our pain and brokenness are not greater than our God; He will not waste one tear your glorious eyes have shed. He will use all of it for His glory, and one day you will share stories not to have someone pick a side, but to point to the God who redeems messy hearts like ours and creates a pretty fantastic sight to behold. People will be drawn to the healed version of you, while the enemy will place distractions for the fractured places in you. Satan does not want you to be whole; he wants you twisted, spilling out your frustrations and harboring unforgiveness.

There are some strategies that have saved my Southern hide in moving forward and making real progress in my life and heart while giving myself permission for a few hot-mess moments when it was safe to rant but not camp out there. You need safe people, and by safe people I mean those who have some serious dirt on you. I'm talking incriminating evidence, sister style. Safe friends cut to the chase, and will call you on the carpet, but know you well enough to understand when it's time to say those things. Sometimes you need lunch with a friend and a nap, and you're going to feel better afterward. During those moments when your heart is hurting, you might not feel like praying, so start by asking God to help you. Talk with your safe person, someone who loves you and who has been a loyal friend.

An unsafe friend is someone who gossips about everyone. If there is trouble and she's often in the middle of it, this is not your safe person. She can't be, because she thrives on chaos and drama. A safe friend lifts your spirits, and you usually feel better after you unload. If *you* are repeating the same story, same issues over and over, girl, you are not a safe person. You are a wounded person, and that's okay. Your safe person is always Jesus. He alone can mend and do what no person or soul sister can do.

The truth about wounds—and I'm speaking from experience on this—is that we always gravitate toward something, and usually those things are unhealthy. My wounds usually require Mexican food or cupcakes, sometimes both. But after my sad lunch turns happier because of comfort food and I've done all the things that make my heart feel loved, I move on. Sometimes I have that hard conversation or send the email after I've sat on it for a while. I make sure my heart and the tone I'm sending out is right. I deal with me because I am only responsible for me. I can't fix my man, my people, my kids, or my dogs, but I love them the best way I know how. I love myself enough to stay in my lane even though I prefer to take up three. If you only knew how hard that is for me. But I try. I go back to the basics.

I scale my life way back and I listen. I tune out the noise of this world. I quiet myself before the Lord and keep it on chill. Sure, I throw some fits, but only for the things that matter. That's it. Not everything is allowed to be fit-worthy.

Scandalous Love

The day after Valentine's Day, I was scheduled to teach at Saving Grace about what else—love. Not just about how to love or what love is, but how to love and care for yourself as a person. Seems easy enough, but there were other factors at play with this subject. Saving Grace is a transitional home for girls who have aged out of the foster care system or who are homeless and need a safe place to call home. Honestly, I knew this would be the hardest class to teach, a room full of girls who have yet to comprehend what healthy love looks like or is. Up until this point they have only seen an imitation of love, a façade in the movies that promises a prince will come and save the day. Most of the love they have known is based on performance and a measuring system that says to be loved you have to throw yourself away, not save your heart and post a guard around it like a fortress that needs to be protected or treated like a hidden treasure waiting to be discovered.

As I began to study for the evening, something came to mind as I began to think about one of the most familiar passages in the Bible on the subject of love. By all accounts, it is completely scandalous, but as I began to read 1 Corinthians 13, this crazy thought entered my mind: What if every woman read this passage and tried to love themselves in this same way? I wondered if we would love better and recognize this kind of love in the ones around us? Or if that realization would help guide all of us who try so stinkin' hard to earn it, to understand that a love like that is so sweet and intense that it requires a relationship with our Creator. The One who fashioned us and loved us and proved it by sending His only Son to die for us. He "so loved" a group of broken girls that He gave it all, His only Son.

A better way to love that heart of yours, inspired by 1 Corinthians 13.

I will be patient with myself, because love is patient.

I will be kind to myself, because love is kind.

I will not envy, boast, or be prideful because love doesn't look like those things.

I will not dishonor myself, because love honors others.

I will not be self-seeking, because I lean into a God whose love abounds and is limitless just because I'm His.

I will not be easily angered with myself, because God is patient and kind to me.

I will not keep a long, long list of all my faults or my record of wrongs, because God loves me. Because He paid for my sins, He freely forgives and doesn't hold them against me, so why should I?

I will protect my heart by being nicer with the words I say to myself.

I will trust God and learn to trust myself again.

I will invite hope into my life again, because love does.

I will persevere because that's what love does.

Love never fails.

God never fails.

I might mess up, but I will never, ever give up because God is on my side. Love is on my side.

Truth Your Soul Needs

God's love is so unwavering, fulfilling, and completing that we don't have to try to earn it or measure up to it. We simply receive it as grace upon grace upon grace. If you want to silence your inner mean girl, try reminding her of what God says about His love. Nothing about God's love for you is based on your performance; it's based on His character. When Scripture tells us how God loved the church so much that He sacrificed His Son, we are told to love that way, too.

When your inner voice sounds like the enemy instead of like love, call it out and make it shut the heck up. If the voice inside your head is unloving, tell her it's time to play nice and practice real love. This will not be easy for those of you who have been beating yourself up for years, but I believe it's time to correct that voice with one that's worth listening to.

Reflective Questions

1. When have you felt the sting of rejection and questioned your worth?
2. Is it time for you to tune out the noise of the world and quiet yourself before the Lord?

Gutsy Prayer

Lord,

I will praise you because you are good. Your love never fails or runs out (Psalms 136:1). I will listen to your truth instead of the doubts that fill my head, and I will trust you with my emotions. When it's easy to fix my eyes on the problems, I will fix my eyes on you, Sovereign Lord; in you I take refuge (Psalm 141:8).

In Jesus' name, amen.

7

The Mending Mindset

Reclaim Your Role as the Leading Lady

ONE OF MY FAVORITE SCENES from the movie *The Holiday* is between an elderly screenwriter, Arthur, and Iris, the brokenhearted British girl who spends her Christmas with strangers trying to get over unrequited love. (The setup: On a whim, two strangers swap homes for the holidays, with Iris trading her quaint little cottage in the English countryside for a posh mansion in Los Angeles. While checking out her new location, she stumbles across Arthur, who is taking a leisurely stroll with his walker and seems hopelessly lost. Iris, kind woman that she is, pulls over to help him find his way home, and from there a relationship develops between strangers from different generations who are both terribly lonely.)

Over dinner one evening, Arthur leans across the table and says, "You know what I've been wondering all night? Why would a beautiful girl like you go to a stranger's house for

Christmas vacation and on top of that, spend Saturday night with . . . me?"

"I just wanted to get away from the people I see all the time. . . . Well, not all the people . . . one person." As Iris begins to cry and wipe her tears, Arthur calls Iris's old beau a schmuck, and when she asks Arthur how he knew that, Arthur replied, "He let you go. This is not a hard one to figure out. Iris, in the movies we have leading ladies, and we have the best friend. You, I can tell, are a leading lady, but for some reason, you are behaving like the best friend."[1]

Bam. Arthur dropped the truth bomb on Iris, and it exploded in her beautiful face. Tears fill her eyes as she says, "You are supposed to be the leading lady of your own life. . . . I've been going to a therapist for three years and she's never explained anything to me that well. That was brilliant. . . . Brutal, but brilliant."[2]

Of all the woven storylines and different characters in this movie, the relationship between Arthur and Iris was my favorite. It's hard not to ask questions when you stumble into a room where an Oscar is being used as a paperweight. What I love most about Arthur is that he was a great storyteller who never lost his spark; he still had a twinkle in his eyes and a wittiness about him. Iris believed she was helping out an old man, but what she didn't realize was that Arthur was helping her out in the way she needed most. This elderly gentleman relived some of his favorite memories from Old Hollywood when he was an award-winning screenwriter while enjoying the company of young Iris—and he noticed something she hadn't: Iris was playing a lesser role than the one she belonged in.

Iris was worth far more than what she was settling for and the lost love she was pining over, but even worse than that, Iris wasn't the leading lady in her own story—her broken heart was. From that moment on, things began to change for Iris. Arthur had already been feeding Iris a steady diet of classic Hollywood movies with leading ladies who had what Arthur called gumption. He knew Iris needed to dig deep to discover she was a gutsy girl and deserved to recast herself as the leading lady. The Oscar winner wasn't just showing Iris movies because she was lonely and bored; he was giving her new material to help her find the spark and gumption that belonged to her.

A schmuck is a schmuck, so why spend more time crying about something or someone who is playing the role of adversary or the one who got away? Leading ladies shine in the role that is uniquely their own. Of course there will be messes, missteps, and tears, with multiple plot twists keeping everyone on their toes, but the real star is the story they wake up and live every day. What Iris thought she needed on Christmas holiday was an escape from her everyday norm and a change in scenery, but what she got was a reset and a shift in her mindset. Iris found her gumption and became a gutsy girl.

The Bumpy Road to Gumption

At the age of twenty-one, bless my ridiculous heart, I was convinced something was wrong with me. Surely God hadn't wired me to be an introvert and yet live a very upfront life in the spotlight of ministry. To be who He had called me to be meant I would have to be someone else, right? Heck to the no. Now in my early forties, I am walking in a chain-breaking freedom after working through my issues with tenacious fortitude through my bless-my-ridiculous-heart twenties and my sweet-merciful-heavens-this-girl-is-finally-getting-it thirties. Instead of a problem to be fix or solved, I am the answer ready to be sharpened and battle-ready. I am ready to listen to the right voices, even if they say a few hard things in love. I am ready to win battles instead of warring in silence on my own.

Starting in my teenage years and into my early twenties, I had learned how to adapt—almost morphing into whoever the person standing in front of me wanted to see. I became a girl jumping through hoops, hoping to earn love based on performance. If I jumped high enough, if I did my best with a smile on my face, everyone would be happy. But I was miserable, sinking in a sea of people-pleasing and missing some of the better things I had to offer.

I had some realistic fears; the data and statistics predicted my future would mirror the familiar brokenness of divorce, alcoholism, and fractured relationships. Flashing lights and warning signs saying I could become what I feared the most—someone unable to hold on to a relationship, unable to hold on to hope, numbing my pain while pretending I was okay. But even as I looked around and saw that did not have to be my reality or my identity, somehow I was still tethered to mistakes I had not made. I was carrying someone else's broken baggage. Those bags did not belong to me, but I had picked up a few like ugly heirlooms and carried a few self-inflicted wounds of my own.

My need for approval followed me into my early years of ministry. Isn't the minister's wife supposed to have it all together even at twenty-two? Um, no. She needs room to grow and stretch like every other twenty-two-year-old. I had so many eyes watching me, so I went to war with the sloppy perfectionist inside of me and released my fear that to be loved I needed to be perfect. I still needed to know that I was enough, even the messy parts of me.

Somewhere along the way, I learned to lay down the baggage that didn't belong to me as I walked in uncharted territories toward wholeness in God.

This is a choice that requires surrender, and it isn't easy, but that doesn't mean it can't be done. Freedom is ours for the taking. But, soul sister, we have to work for it.

Something profound happened when I finally embraced a moving-on mindset: Freedom would look a lot like changing my mindset to mirror the promises of God. ***The Holy Spirit will always be more powerful than the moments that try to break us.***

Deep within my threadbare places, a blazing hope consumed my timid, insecure heart. I believed that God could use a girl who didn't have it all together. The first (and biggest) thing I had to discard to move forward in my life was my pride.

In the past, my inner craving for belonging became a mask to hide behind, a chain around my heart, crippling the gifts that God had placed inside. But He came to set me free—not part of the way, not just-barely-getting-by free—but free indeed. His freedom is so sweet, so satisfying, and it's paid for: no jumping through hoops required. You open your hands and heart and receive the gift He wants so much for you to have.

A few years ago I felt slapped with an approval rating in one of my close-knit relationships; it was a pretty low score, actually, and it hurt me deeply. It reached beyond playing a role to an intensely personal level that reopened old wounds from not feeling good enough in the past. Before, I might have spiraled into a pit of depression and accepted this score, but thankfully growing in your faith gives you room to reject things that might otherwise destroy you and your self-worth. We have a choice about what we are going to take into our hearts and carry around with us. Unconditional love doesn't come with a scorecard and a measuring system. Our choice is to travel light. We might have to throw a few things away and unpack our bags from time to time, but we will not throw away our confidence.

I want to walk with you on this journey and introduce you to a way to move forward in life and live beyond the breakthrough. Freedom—and moving forward—means no longer fixating on problems, choosing instead to dwell on the promises of God. This is what living faith forward truly is: changing our expectations to reflect who God is in our lives instead of what we are experiencing or feeling in the natural. We trade our victim mentality for a warrior mentality that is victorious even when the battle is long and hard.

> **Gumption (n.):** nerve, bravery, moxie, grit, initiative, resourcefulness, fortitude, strength of mind, backbone, guts. "The quality of being sensible and brave enough to do the right thing in a difficult situation."[3]
>
> **Used in a sentence:** It takes gumption to get things done.

Shoot, yeah, it does. But moving forward in our lives takes a lot more than just gumption. When our willpower merges with God's supernatural power, we have something far greater than personal fortitude; we have freedom. But not just any kind of freedom—the kind of freedom that makes the devil yell, "That wild Jesus girl is at it again!" Life is hard, and we are all getting over something or in the process of it, but the impetus for us as believers is going into spiritual battle with better tools. By changing our thoughts and how we look at the things that have happened to us, we can change our lives and have victory now and in the future.

> It is for freedom that Christ has set us free. Stand firm, then, and do not let yourselves be burdened again by a yoke of slavery.
>
> Galatians 5:1

This is a common pattern for all of us; if it wasn't, we wouldn't have this passage in Galatians giving us a heads-up and telling us to gird our loins, hoist up our womanhood with a push-up bra that supports us in all the right places . . . or stand firm. Whatever, you get the point. Instead of returning to the scene of the crime and to the things that have held us in bondage for so long, we stand in the strength God has for us. Often, we return to what is comfortable without realizing it is the very thing that has crippled us from growing stronger and is what keeps us from finding freedom in our lives.

Steps Toward Unstuck

What is it that keeps you stuck?

What is your emotional equivalent of a comfort blanket with an old pattern that has you stagnant instead of striding forward in life?

Restoration of your mind and soul starts with making a pact with your Maker to seek His plan more than ____________ ____________________.

Broken girls play the victim. Healed girls fight for victory armed with the truth. I don't have to tell you what was "done" to me. But I will, with all my gutsy strength, point to the One who breathed new life into me. Whole girls know victory is their everyday destiny. Even when they can't see it in the natural, the gutsy heart inside of them reminds them that freedom is already theirs and it is good.

To reclaim the power of your story, you first have to accept that it belongs to you and no one else. It's yours. Nothing about brokenness has to be passive. While we fear we are stuck, we have already met the solution and remedy for every problem and sickness of the soul: Jesus.

It's okay for us to call our brokenness what it is—a bad hand that was dealt to us or a bump in the road where our muffler gets left behind in the small town we never belonged in called Stuckville. We don't move there or camp out; we pass through it. How we think about our problems reveals everything.

By changing your thoughts, you can change your life:

- People are not capable of being your source; only Jesus can be your source.
- We cannot expect flawed people to fix us.
- Co-dependency isn't a good option, but God-dependency is.
- Our confidence cannot be stolen from us, only given and discarded with our permission.

> So do not throw away your confidence; it will be richly rewarded.
>
> Hebrews 10:35

Remember, "almost free" isn't freedom at all. It is a trick the enemy uses to hold us captive with a counterfeit liberty that leaves us soul-starved. Our worth and value do not have to be tied to the bottomless pit of people-pleasing. We don't have to throw away our confidence or dumpster-dive for the blessings of others. Instead of throwing away our confidence, we do the opposite. We fight for it and dare not let go. That is gumption, my friend; that is pure gutsiness and the furthest thing from defeat and passivity.

Let's practice a little gumption, shall we?

- You, ____________________, are not my source. Jesus is.
- You don't get to measure me, scale on my cold bathroom floor and my stretched-out waistline. You can fluctuate all you want, but my worth never will.

- You don't get to control me, comfort food or __________________.
- You, ______________________, cannot steal my confidence or worth because it's God-given, not man-given. I don't need you to affirm me any longer.
- From this day forward, _____________________, you are fired from being the standard against which I measure myself.

Truth Your Soul Needs

Your Worth

A mirror cannot show you it.

A man cannot assure you of it.

A magazine cannot strip you of it.

Your past cannot deny you of it.

The Moving-on Mindset

- We press on and lay hold of what God has for us. This is actively moving forward in our actions and our thought life.
- We choose to forget and no longer waste our thoughts on the past, but reach forward. This act is a continual pressing, actively moving toward God and His plan for us.

> Not that I have already obtained all this, or have already arrived at my goal, but I press on to take hold of that for which Christ Jesus took hold of me. Brothers and sisters, I do not consider myself yet to have taken hold of it. But one thing I do: Forgetting what is behind

> and straining toward what is ahead, I press on toward the goal to win the prize for which God has called me heavenward in Christ Jesus.
>
> Philippians 3:12–14

Reflective Questions

1. Are you starring in your life as leading lady, playing a supporting role, or walking through your life as an extra?
2. Do you have an Arthur in your life who cares enough about you to feed you new material? (If you can't identify a person, know that we all have one in Jesus, whose powerful Word provides the script!)
3. What landed you in Stuckville? How do you need to change your thinking about that event, circumstance, or mindset in order to move on?

Gutsy Prayer

Lord,

My heart is weary from feeling stuck. I want to not only take ownership of my story, I want to see your glory in it. Lead me to the rock that is higher than I, for you have been my refuge, a strong tower against the enemy (Psalm 61:2–3). I know that you have plans to prosper me and not to harm me, to give me hope and a future (Jeremiah 29:11). Thank you for the people you have placed in my life to lead me closer to you.

In Jesus' name, amen.

8

The Price of Breakthrough

HEY, DON'T COUNT YOURSELF out just yet. I know it hurts right now, but this is how warriors are made. It's kind of like when you have birthing pains and you beg for something to numb it. Everything inside of you wants to quit, but somehow you push through the pain because you were designed to carry the most important and beautiful things in life to the other side of that pain. There is a place on the other side of it, and it's worth the ache to get you there. It always hurts most right before your biggest breakthrough. But out of that pain comes something worth fighting for: You become someone you're proud of and you have a greater understanding of your worth. You were the prize all along, the hidden treasure you've been digging for in the dark. You don't have to claw anymore to prove your worth; go wash and ready your hands to receive your new assignment. The battle you've been fighting has already been won and paid for in full. In the words of my friend and editor Kim Bangs, "Warrior up, baby."

The price of breakthrough isn't just my story; it's all of ours. What happens when women share their breakthrough stories with the world? Further healing takes place in the heart of the one sharing and in the hearts of those listening. They become a part of your breakthrough story, too. They become the women cheering you on along the way. I think the earth is going to shake a little as chains fall from hands and feet. When we find freedom, we give others permission to do the same.

I have the sweetest little community of gutsy girls who have become my tribe. And in the pages of this book, I am honored to share a few of their stories. Friends, meet some new members of our tribe.

Warrior Mom to Many: Becky Shaffer's Gutsy Girl Story

Becky Shaffer walked through the hallway of Saving Grace with a rekindled mission in her heart. In her hands she held anointing oil—not just any anointing oil, but a unique blend that was made for her by her oldest daughter. Becky is a warrior who grew up and raised warrior daughters surrounded by prayer and an honest mother who wasn't afraid to let them see her for who she was: a mother in the process of mending.

Becky grew up in foster care, but before she ended up there, she was mothered by a woman with mental illness who left gaping holes and fractures in her young mind. But that's only part of her story. This past year had been extremely painful for Becky. Why? Because you can't take back enemy territory—by holding a safe, sacred space at the table for young women with similar stories—without the enemy using you for target practice.

Being a CEO isn't easy, but if you want to know what true success looks like, I'll point you to the mission and heartbeat behind Saving Grace, a transitional home for young women ages seventeen to twenty-five who have aged out of the foster care system or group homes, are facing homelessness, or have been abandoned by critical support. These young women show up in need of a tribe of their own and yet have no true understanding of what a healthy tribe and family looks like.

Becky doesn't want any of the credit for Saving Grace, and she doesn't want to be applauded. It's not possible for her to even receive it; trust me, we all have tried. She will point upward and tell you to praise the God who saved her. But what Becky has allowed God to do in her, and through her team at Saving Grace, makes the enemy fighting mad. Like the punk he is, he will always target you in the area where you have made the most progress. So instead of feeling surrounded by support during the past year, Becky was questioning everything, including who she could trust in life. It's what recovering broken girls do: We go back to our broken beginning until one day we've forgotten that we were broken in the first place.

After a sabbatical, Becky showed up ready to pray over meetings and over the women she was not only serving with but leading to a new season of breakthrough. For a year she had been in a silent battle, but when you are in leadership, your private life becomes unfortunately public. Yet Becky Shaffer was back and walking in a new power after a humbling and heartbreaking season; she was ready to be empowered to do the hard task of leading, and was going in armed with prayer.

Just as Becky made it to the doorway of the room she was about to pray fire down in, the anointing oil slipped out of her hands and the container shattered on the floor. Anointing oil and broken glass were everywhere. Becky told me that she bent down and said, "Stupid devil, you just anointed everything." And then she put her hands in oil and began to anoint the room with prayer. Everything inside of her knew that moment was a tipping point, one that would have made her give up during the last year of wrestling—but not this time. The oil wasn't damaged. She was not damaged. The work God had called her to wasn't damaged. Only the container that held the oil was damaged, but her spirit was stronger than ever. Nothing was unused that day, certainly not the special oil made for her by someone she loved. Nothing was wasted; shards of glass couldn't stop the fragrant smell of the anointing oil and one woman's determination to pray through to her breakthrough. But this wasn't her first rodeo and experience with breakthrough. Becky shared the following with readers in a letter on her blog to offer more of her story and to encourage others working with foster care and transitional living.

Transformed from a Broken Girl to a Gutsy Girl

Mama would always give us a spoon of dry oatmeal and drink of milk so that when we were asked by the caseworker what we had for breakfast, we would not have to lie. Mama convinced us that if we told anyone we didn't have anything to eat that caseworker would take us away, and we would be split up and never see each other again. Eventually, my three older siblings ran from home one by one. My mother was always violent with my oldest sister. I was only seven when she finally ran; it would be years before I saw her again. Mama then turned her rage on me. She often would place a box fan in the bedroom window and have me strip down to my panties, and she would beat me until she was too exhausted to continue.

I would wait until the coast was clear and go out to the backyard and lie in the grass and talk to God. I never felt alone during my mother's storms. . . . I always felt His presence and knew it would be okay. As I prayed while the tears were still drying on my little cheeks, I'd ask God for a new family, one that would love me and keep me safe, with a mom, dad, brothers, and sisters, and horses. I grew older and taller and began to fight back, but mostly through running and becoming involved with the wrong crowd. At the age of twelve, I found myself in and out of jail, at a detention center. I ran away and ended up back in jail. Mrs. Brewer, my caseworker, would threaten to send me to Pine Bluff, Arkansas, but thankfully she sent me to a children's home in Oklahoma instead.

I arrived at the children's home on a Wednesday afternoon. I was checked in at the office where I met my foster-mother. She took me in an old mint-green van back to the cottage that I would soon call home. I was terrified at first, but not after meeting the other children, including my roommate who was fifteen. She was awesome and put me at ease instantly. Barbie taught me two priceless things, how to laugh and how to whistle, both of which I'm good at. After I put my few things away, we ate dinner, soup and sandwiches; it is etched in my mind like it was yesterday. As I went to bed that night, I thanked God for all the things He'd given me that I'd asked for so many years before.

I graduated from high school in 1988 and knew I had to figure out what I was going to do as there was not one place for me to go after graduation. I decided to go to college, and when I moved to Dallas to attend Dallas Christian College, I was there because I needed a place to live. While other freshman students were wondering if they were going to make it for class at seven in the morning, I was wondering what I would do for the holidays.

Due to my own story and watching the girls who lived in my home when I became a foster parent who became a part of our little family not having options as they aged out, my husband and I started a transitional living house in Rogers that has fourteen bedrooms for young women aging out or homeless.

You must at times wonder if what you are doing is making a difference . . . it is. Don't stop pressing on and doing the hard work. I have such respect for you and personally want to work with you to change the future to break the silent epidemic in our nation and help heal the hearts of our children and break the cycle of abuse and neglect and a life of poverty.

Becky Shaffer, founder and CEO of Saving Grace NWA[1]

Wildly Free: Melissa Blair's Gutsy Girl Story

My friend Melissa Blair looks like freedom. When she is in the room, I sit back and enjoy the show because I know it is bound to be a good one. She is not only charming and terribly funny, she is also deeply rooted in faith and speaks with such wisdom. When she talks about Jesus, you see a fire in her eyes and find yourself hanging on every word, even the ones she hasn't said yet. She has been through fire and crippling defeat, but I believe Melissa is going to change the world. Years ago, the inner turmoil in her head was a tug-of-war between grace and accusations. She sat in a pew each Sunday feeling the sting of shame from a decision she made when she was a teenager. Raise your hand if you did something Fifty Shades of Stupid as a teenager. That's what I thought: All hands go up, including mine.

Sin is sin. Yet we place sins in different categories, as big and little, really bad and not so bad. But it's all bad because sin is sin. We try to clean up the things that are tarnished and sin-stained, but we have all fallen short of the glory of God (Romans 3:23). Not some of us—all of us.

Something profound happened to this girl who lights up every room she walks into: In the deepest places of her secret shame, she found the power of her testimony and said in front of 1.5 million women watching with stories just like hers, "to hell with shame."

The price of breakthrough is the pain you feel beforehand, but the prize is the glorious freedom that you want to tell the whole world about. Freedom is contagious, but so are bad moods. Can I get an amen? The pain is always more unbearable right before the shift in your heart and happenings collide. Sometimes the actual circumstance changes and you feel some form of relief, but most of the time the prize of breakthrough is a noticeable change in heart—a new attitude and a new lifestyle that is yours, not someone else's. I watched my friend Melissa find the courage to share one of the moments in her life that changed everything for her. It was the day she believed God loved her so deeply and personally that she set aside the decade-long shame-slinging and shared a part of her story, and in the process she found freedom that is life-changing and grace-giving. As a result, God has used her beyond her wildest dreams to help women with similar stories throat-punch shame and tell it exactly where to go.

I read Melissa's letter to her sixteen-year-old self and wept, and with her permission, I share it with you now because

Melissa Blair not only is living beyond breakthrough, but her life and who she is as a woman is a prize we all get to enjoy and celebrate.

A Letter to My Sixteen-Year-Old Self

Hey girl,

Listen. I need to talk to you. It's not about the hole in the ozone you're singlehandedly responsible for because of the Aqua Net in that perm of yours or that you need to forgive your dad earlier and love him better because he won't always be around.

This is serious.

And it will change the way you walk for the rest of your life. So, get some coffee (you'll be addicted by college anyway) and have a seat, okay?

You'll soon read a story in high school English about a young woman who was forced by her community to wear the scarlet letter A *to show her sin of adultery to the world. The marking on her dress, along with her public shaming, was her punishment for her sin and her secrecy. You read it as a strange fiction at the time, disconnected and far-fetched from real life. But not too long after that class ends, you will begin to live out your days marked by your own secret* A*, and it will make perfect sense.*

There will be a season in your life you split your time between friends, playing every sport, or learning how to drive. You will fall for a boy who says he loves you. That desire to feel loved will pull you out to sea, away from solid ground, and drown you whole. I wish I could change the story here for you, but you will find yourself pregnant.

You'll soon figure out you're on your own in this one. With a daddy's words about shame if he ever finds you in this boat ringing in your ears and the sight of the boy you loved with his arm around his new girl, you will feel like you don't have a choice.

But you do.

And you did.

You will make the decision to have an abortion.

It will be easier than you thought it would . . . or should be. You'll walk into the clinic expecting to defend or beg for your decision, hoping no one would try and talk you out of it and also wishing someone would. You needn't have worried: there will be no care about why you're there, nor comfort or even eye contact.

Just a signature here with a fake name and discharge directions advising against basketball practice for 72 hours. You'll go back to school on Monday and almost hemorrhage yourself into the hospital in math class but just wait for the death that will surely come at home because you don't want to wear that scarlet letter now, do you?

And you don't tell anyone.

And you live to see another day.

Sort of.

Because life will be different for you now.

You will wake up one morning a mostly whole young woman and go to sleep that same night as a different half-dead version of yourself.

This will not change for more than twenty years.

One day you'll sit on the edge of the bed and tell the good man you married about that day so long ago at the tender prompting of a God you barely knew.

You'll brace yourself for the disappointment you deserve to carry for what you did.

And it will never come.

He will hold you and tell you how sorry he is and how much he loves you. He will never mention it again for all the years and you'll begin to wonder if he forgot what you told him. This will be your first experience with Jesus in this terrible story.

There will be many times you sit in a church service and listen to the pastor discuss how the murdering of babies is a sin. You'll wonder for just a breath if there's still someone who doesn't know that. You'll concentrate on a cellular level for your body to not twitch or move in reaction to this still-bleeding wound being publicly probed. You'll feel the heat rising in both cheeks like two red guilty stains that give you away and imagine everyone is staring at you.

You'll leave church with a heart more tangled and confused than it was coming in that morning.

For a long time, you will feel you don't have a right to be pro-life. After all, you made the wrong choice. You feel like a hypocrite participating in the walks or conversations for awareness or your desire to talk to women about your devastating experience with abortion.

So, you don't and you sit quietly with a soul groaning to speak up.

But after you've grown a bit, you might start to notice that the people who have maybe the most right to talk about how dangerous a fire can be are the ones you can see whose skin has melted from the flames. They're the ones you tend to listen to in life anyway and not the ones who care more about the fact that there's a fire than the people getting burned up inside it.

There will come a season that you fall madly in love with Christ with the full functioning capacity of the half of your heart you allowed to live past sixteen. And He, calling us deeper still into love, will whisper one morning in the quiet:

It's time.

You'll understand what He means and you'll be scared. But more than the fear? You feel relieved. He'll send you a sister who walked her own different but still broken road and lived to see the spacious freedom on the other side that only those who understand the dark-honest depth of their need get to experience. She'll hold your confession tender in her hands and whisper true things in your ear that shed light on things long hidden.

Just like your husband, just like Jesus:

You will be exposed heart-naked and human as the day you were born . . . and fully loved anyway.

This will begin to breathe a new kind of life into the deadest parts of you. Once again and sweeter still, life will be different for you now. And while you would change this part of your story in a single heartbeat, you would never give back one inch of knowing this kind of amazing grace.

You'll own freedom in a different way after the wound in your soul begins to close up, but I also need to warn you: you'll still have to defend it, fight to believe it some days. There will be this thing called the internet and a week will never go by without your scarlet letter being called out. You'll take the stones thrown in social media venting about abortion and you'll feel confused by the church you love, mad for the women being alienated with harsh words, and sad for the unborn babies none of this is helping.

And you'll stay offline for grace and peace's sake.

You'll think there is a better way for the body of Christ to advocate for the life of the unborn, to be a safe place for girls who think they have no choice, and to also heal the bondage of shame for women like you who made the decision to have an abortion. You believe the silence forced on women who have the capacity to change the conversation will be deafening and a blow to the defense of life. But you feel like admitting any of this will earn you a lettered dress forever.

You'll mourn for the one out of every three women who hemorrhage their shame in private because, as we all find out, death is often preferable to judgment. The church will hurt, but it's also where you find your healing so you'll need to forgive and love like your Jesus does. Christ took away your letter and put it on Himself just for you, girl. So, your response will be to live a life of gratitude.

One last thing before I go?

One night you're going to come home from confessing the twenty-plus-year-old shame you've gotten used to shackling to your own leg to a bunch of women from different churches. Because practicing the freedom you already own is still new for you, you're going to drive away with tears falling into your lap singing to God with one side of your mouth and cussing with the other side at the anguish it takes to put words around this part of your story. When you get home, your precious husband will ask you, "How'd it go?"

You'll pause too long and your eyes will flood all over again. He takes you in, he tells you it's good, it's all so good.

"This is God's story and He already took care of that, Baby."

God is good to send others to tell us the things we sometimes forget to remember. It's just one of the ways He gets to wrap His arms around us while we are here and whisper low and sweet deep down in our ears:

"I see you and I fully know you. You are mine, sweet girl, and you are loved.

I exchanged every letter of yours for My own life. Now go live, and love others, like you believe Me."

You'll keep finding out over and over that vulnerability is usually scary, courage often follows obedience, and that this story is not about you.

And one day you'll decide to believe Him and you'll want that freedom for others even more than you want it for yourself . . .

and you'll write yourself a letter.

I'm sorry to keep you so long. I know you have basketball practice, but this just couldn't wait another minute. Take care. And go a little easier on your parents, okay? One day you're going to see how much grace they really needed.

Love,
Me[2]

The Wrestle

Melissa is in our little tribe called the Word Girls, in northwest Arkansas. Once a month we meet with this amazing group of women in ministry. It's not possible for all of us to make it to every meeting, so we don't always get to see each other often, but when we do we make it count. There are usually a handful of things said between safe friends that are utterly ridiculous. By ridiculous, I mean hilarious. Then the conversation shifts to God and the pursuit of Him with every fiber of who we are. In our forties, we can be both rooted deeply in our faith and utterly ridiculous. We are 100 percent okay with that because we've fought hard to like who we've become.

I become quiet and listen to my friends seated around the table. That's what we do best: We listen to the words that haven't been spoken yet. And sometimes I say the brave words for them, and they say mine for me.

A few months ago, I found myself fangirling another friend who has been a woman underneath the controlling thumb of another person for most of her life. The men she loved most required her to be small and less. Heaven forbid if somewhere in the space of manipulative abuse she actually figured out that she was destined for more—that she is worth all the kind words any good-hearted man can find and all the ones he can't. When I told her that she was the proud owner of her story and that she could tell it any way she wanted, she shook her head and said, "I made a vow to honor him in public. I fear God and know I will be accountable for every word."

I, on the other hand, wanted to hunt him down and pummel him multiple times as I watched my friend lay to rest the death of her abusive marriage and learn to stand taller than her five-foot-three frame allows. What kind of woman honors a dishonorable man? A godly woman who wrestled in the dark alone and found out on her own that she is anything but small and unworthy. Whether the abuse is from words or angry hands, calling abuse what it is can be scary, because manipulation points to the abused and tells us that it was our fault, that somehow we deserved it. But not anymore: We won't be held underneath a heavy hand of reckless words.

Women who pursue Jesus and healing are bound to figure out their worth eventually. My friend did, and she is free. But still I sometimes see this strong woman in ministry, an incredible mother and friend, take a backseat in the car she's supposed to be driving. Let me just brag about her though, because she is in the driver's seat 90 percent of the time now; I'm just gutsy enough to push for that last 10 percent for her. I'm gutsy enough to push for the last ten for all of us. I call out this behavior in both of us over a casual meal because even as women who have been set free, we sometimes apologize politely for believing we are worth more than we have been led to believe in the past, and we dismiss the destiny that is rightfully ours.

"But why do we still do this?" I ask but don't wait long enough for the answer.

"As good little firstborn broken girls, we have even given God an out to His promises. It's time for us to not do that." My strong reply hung in the air, taking even me by surprise.

God doesn't need an out. He needs us to believe Him.

Did Jacob apologize for wrestling in the dark for his blessing and duking it out with an angel? Uh, no. He refused to let go, his death grip overpowering the angel. Do I think that angel could have whipped him? I sure do. But I think gutsy desperation and reaching out for blessing deserves a reward. The other side of that means a blessing of such magnitude requires an exhausting wrestling match before we get the breakthrough we need. We stop short because wrestling is hard; we say pretty please, then let go right before our miracle happens. Most of the time we are looking for something to hold in our hands, visible proof of an answered prayer and the things we long for.

We are taking the backseat when it comes to living our lives and owning our stories, and I'm not sure that's a good thing. It's one thing when we allow Jesus to take the wheel, but it's another when we forfeit our keys because someone wants to control us. Jesus isn't like that. He laid down His life for us and wants an invitation into our lives with a seat right next to us. He wants all of us. The wet tears at His feet, the hot mess, and costly (or cheap) perfume we pour over Him as a gift. Whatever you have is exactly what Jesus wants.

In Genesis 32:22 we find Jacob sending his two wives, his two female servants, and his eleven sons over a brook while he is left alone. With two wives and eleven sons, I can't imagine the noise level and madness that came from so many voices, so many needs, and only one of him. Lord knows that man needed some personal space. Jacob, whose name meant *deceiver*, needed to be all alone in the dark to meet with God face-to-face.

It's hard to be the ones who wrestle. And yet, deeper purpose runs through us, transforming us, when we have been left alone to wrestle in the dark. Sometimes all we need to do is get out of the way and let God do His thing. We grasp aimlessly at the nothingness, wanting a sword or whatever we can place in our hands to fight off the enemy of our souls, our destiny, and our name-change moment. Yet in Jacob's empty-handed moment, it was just two strong hands against another's in face-to-face combat.

"Then Jacob was left alone; and a Man wrestled with him until the breaking of day" (Genesis 32:24 NKJV). And the Man could not prevail; this angel of the Lord had to throw Jacob's hip out of joint.

Angel: "Let me go, for the day breaks."

Jacob: "I will not let you go unless you bless me."

"What is your name?"

"My name is Deceiver."

"That's not your name anymore. This is your name: Israel; for you have wrestled with God and with men, and have prevailed."

My friend, your name has been changed, too. You are no longer the walking wounded—you are a gutsy girl who looks like freedom. You are not afraid to wrestle and you don't tiptoe around the promises of God; you are fierce enough to wrestle it out with your Maker and walk away blessed. The wrestle is always worth it. The wrestle is what makes us great. But it's lonely, isn't it? Yet that process of becoming who we are, when it's just us and Jesus in a slug-fest, is our greatest untold story. One day you won't have to be so fearful and careful when you share your story with others.

To be set free we must first admit that we are not. Those who limp fly higher than those who avoid divine wrestling matches. God is waiting to change your name to "favored one" and to change you into someone who is too big to fit underneath a thumb (Psalm 5:12). Wrestle for that 10 percent, or whatever your percentage is. The wrestle is worth the end result of freedom and blessing.

But know that your wrestle is not with the person who hurt you and made you smaller. Don't settle for "almost whole." Soul-satisfying rewards are a direct result of your wrestle when you make a commitment, like Jacob, to not let go until you feel blessings from God, exchanging timidity and fear for empowerment from on high.

> For God has not given us a spirit of fear, but of power and of love and of a sound mind.
>
> 2 Timothy 1:7 NKJV

Truth Your Soul Needs

You, my friend, are a gutsy girl. Sure, it hurts the most before your breakthrough, but the life you long to live is worth the hard work you are doing now. Sometimes your circumstances actually change, releasing you from the pressure you had been experiencing before, but most of the time the real prize of breakthrough is the noticeable change in heart, a lifestyle of walking in freedom that belongs to you. Brave women shared their very personal stories of breakthrough with you. What's your Gutsy Girl story?

Jacob had to wrestle with God and walk with a permanent limp to become Israel. He did it because he trusted God with what he had yet to receive from the Lord. But Jacob refused to let go until he had the blessing he desired most. And that fighting spirit paid off for him, just like it will for us. I believe the key to living out our wildest dreams is having a wild, risky prayer life and a gutsy willingness to fight for it. Praying bold prayers and coming to Christ expectantly will change our hearts and lead us to abundant living.

Reflective Questions

1. What is your Gutsy Girl story?
2. Who could you bless by sharing your story?
3. For what are you willing to wrestle with God?

Gutsy Prayer

Lord,

I want to be a Gutsy Girl and share my story with those who need to hear it most. Teach me how to wrestle for the right things and for the blessings you have for me, like Jacob did. Help me to not let go until I feel the shift in my heart and walk away blessed and provided for.

In Jesus' name, amen.

9

You Are the Catalyst to the Breakthrough You Are Looking For

I CALLED MY PRAYER WARRIOR Ruth right before an important meeting yesterday. My tribe was praying. I had been diligently praying, but I needed to hear Ruth pray. This girl is a fireball. Ruth finished praying and then said, "Jennifer, people are going to ask you for a formula. You don't have one, or I would ask you for it and you would be rich. Just give them Jesus." No, I don't have a formula, but I can still see our symptoms and that there's a reason for them.

I became incredibly bored with the broken-girl label I was wearing years ago, so I had a straight-up Holy Ghost breakthrough to rip off my victim label. I was not walking in freedom—I was fixated on all the wrong things and looking back instead of moving forward with hope. I have the answer, not a formula. It's Jesus. It's taking Him at His word. It's a stubborn refusal to give up until you are set free and healed on the inside. Four friends took the stairs, uncovered a roof, and lowered a paralytic man through it to meet his healer in Mark 2:1–5. If we are brutally honest with each other, we would admit that we all want an easy fix to our problems. Four friends refused to let a crowded room deter their faith and the need of their broken friend. Four people did heavy lifting so one man could take up his mat and walk free and forgiven.

We don't have a formula; we have Jesus and a gutsy faith that's unafraid to rip up a roof, or anything else standing in our way. Real freedom and spiritual breakthrough is hard work, gutsy faith, and heavy lifting. It's so worth it. Keep going. Get a little messy. Take the stairs.

Ask for the Holy Spirit to open your eyes to see your answer, and don't be afraid to work hard for it. It will be worth it, you'll see. Keep going, sweet friend.

"Who Will I Be If I Stay?"

One of my favorite movies is *Wonder Woman*.[1] The beautifully dynamic, kick-butt Diana is the Wonder Woman we all secretly, or not-so-secretly, want to be. I have a real problem after every superhero movie I walk out of: I am convinced that I could scissor-kick anyone three times my size in the face and live to tell about it. I forget I'm actually five feet four, forty-two, and *slightly* out of shape. The truth is, I feel strong on the inside because I've worked hard to find the kind of strength in Christ that isn't limited by the boxes we often put ourselves in.

Diana grew up with fierce warrior women to glean and learn from, and an overprotective mother who knew her true identity. And because her mother knew what she was destined for, she chose to hide her. *Let that sink in for a minute while you realize that you might be hiding your true identity, too.* Isn't that what we do? The very thing that makes us great and stand out is also the place we harbor insecurity and lies from the enemy telling us to hide what God intends to use for His glory. Your true identity scares the enemy of your soul. But it also scares you because you don't think that powerful identity belongs to you. Wonder Woman is fierce and fabulous, but she has nothing on you, my warrior sister.

Diana had an aunt who saw the undeniable spark inside of her for greatness, but beyond that moxie was Diana's greatest strength: She was teachable and had a determination to not quit. Diana's aunt pushed her to test her limits and trained her to become the warrior she was meant to be.

As the story progresses, you can see the shift from a training period and set of physical tests for Diana to a time of becoming armed and ready for the battle she was born to fight. Diana sets out to stop World War I, believing the conflict was started by the longtime enemy of the Amazons. Diana decides to leave at dark, hoping to set sail while her mother and her people were sound asleep. But what Diana didn't know is that moms have a special radar and compass in their soul. We find out all the things we need to know; it doesn't matter who you are. Diana's mother was already waiting for her, aware that Diana was going to fight the forces of evil, despite all of her fears. In a scene that ripped out my heart and punched me in the face, Diana's mother told her that she had been the greatest love of her life. But on that night, Diana became her mother's greatest pain. As her mother tells Diana what she already knows—that once Diana leaves she can never return—Diana says, with tears in her eyes, "But who will I be if I stay?"

Who will you be if you stay, if you hide and play it safe? Who will you turn out to be if you decide it's too much work and the effort isn't worth it—because you're convinced you are not worth it? Do you really want to find that out? There is a warrior princess inside of you right now. Sister, I didn't just write this book for you, I ripped up a roof to lower you down for this moment. I have prayed for each heart reading this message. I have prayed for the women you will reach and the lives you will touch. I will continue to do the heavy lifting because I know you are worth it.

You are the catalyst to the breakthrough you have been longing for. It's there inside of you—the teachable determination that gives me great hope that you are not stuck. You are becoming battle ready. You are the hero of your own story. With Jesus alive and active in your heart, you have everything you need. So what are you waiting on? *Warrior up, baby.*

Soul Strategy

I can handle whatever the enemy throws at me because I never handle it on my own. I can do all things through Jesus Christ who gives me strength (Philippians 4:13).

I don't have to freak out and react to everything, because the Lord almighty is my source of strength and my portion.

> My flesh and my heart may fail, but God is the strength of my heart and my portion forever.
>
> Psalm 73:26

I am allowed to have off days and make mistakes, because I know the Lord can use those trip-ups to show me His steadfast love and faithfulness.

> The steadfast love of the Lord never ceases; his mercies never come to an end; they are new every morning; great is your faithfulness.
>
> Lamentations 3:22–23 ESV

I am not a hot mess all the time; I am a new creation in Christ Jesus, and He who began a good work in me will be faithful to complete it!

Jesus wants to empower you, but the enemy wants to hold you captive.

> Therefore, if anyone is in Christ, the new creation has come: The old has gone, the new is here!
>
> 2 Corinthians 5:17

> Being confident of this, that he who began a good work in you will carry it on to completion until the day of Christ Jesus.
>
> Philippians 1:6

Can I confess that of all the things I thought were holding me back in the past, the real issue and the biggest obstacle in my way was me? The way I thought about my circumstances and issues was my personal, jacked-up kryptonite. It weakened any chance I had for progress because I refused to stop dwelling on the past and had a mindset that crippled me and left me stuck. We cannot fight the real enemy of our soul if we are too busy and preoccupied beating ourselves up. Sometimes we feed the bears; we enable toxic people to ruin our day and allow destructive thoughts in our head to take over and fill up our precious heart and mind.

We are far more powerful than we even realize, but only when we lean on Jesus as our source. He will help us take thoughts captive and guide us as we go to battle with the bad habits and patterns that have become our norm. Freedom looks a lot like partnering with the Holy Spirit and calling out the things you know are harmful to your spiritual growth. You, my friend, are a warrior with a soft heart and hands. You are breaking rank and going straight to the source of strength for winning those bloody battles. God is not only with you; God is for you!

"You gotta do what you gotta do."

My youngest daughter, Elise, had been ill for an entire week. After she vomited for two days, I took her to the doctor and was told it was just a virus that needed to run its course. The only problem with that advice is that when my petite girl gets sick, it completely wipes her out. She was only five or six at the time, and she was skin and bones after a week of nonstop vomiting and other fun stuff. When she became extremely weak and lethargic, I picked up my baby and told my husband, Jonathan, to meet us at the hospital and to bring a change of clothes for Elise. Our family had been visiting that week from out of state, but I spent the majority of that time away from everyone, caring for my baby, freeing up Jonathan and our older daughter, Whitley, to enjoy our family. I'm one of those mothers who nurtures with every fiber of who I am. When my babies are sick, they are my primary concern and priority. They are always my first priority, but when they are sick, I am by their side 24/7.

Sometimes it is the most helpless feeling knowing that all I can do is be on the cleanup crew and make their favorite homemade chicken noodle soup. I can't heal them. If I could, I would. But I can be there to help in whatever ways I can and to snuggle with them as much as they will let me. I'll admit, I was all the way over projectile vomiting and smelling like it (and worse). But you pull your hair back and roll up your sleeves, grab a butt-load of Clorox wipes, and pray to Jesus you don't start vomiting, too.

In the ER, I found myself fighting back the tears as the nurses tried multiple times to find a vein in Elise's tiny little arm, but she was so dehydrated by then they couldn't. They were determined to get the IV in and had multiple nurses trying after the others failed. As I brushed Elise's blond hair out of her face, I whispered to her, "Baby, I am so sorry. You are doing so good."

She raised her frail arms up, making her tiny hands into fists, and said, "You gotta do what you gotta do." *Yes, you do, baby. Yes, you do.*

She might have been severely weakened, but her spirit was fierce and brave. After multiple tries, all three of us were crying—Mom, Dad, and baby girl. As the doctor began to tell us what to do next to get her hydrated, we started pushing liquids in small doses and praying for them to work. After a few hours, the doctor released us and reminded us how vital it was to continue giving the fluids a tablespoon at a time until Elise was hydrated again. Her motivation was this: I will do whatever it takes to not have needles in my arms. Our motivation was to get her well by watching the clock and pushing those liquids even when she was utterly annoyed with us for disturbing her favorite Disney movie on repeat.

Elise was on to something huge: How she felt about what she was going through was key. She didn't have to like it, but she wanted to be well, and even though her arms hurt and were covered in Band-Aids, it was just something she had to do. But when the doctor told Elise that she would get better if she just kept those liquids in a little at a time, consistently, she was all in for making that happen and not having to wear an ugly nightgown that opened in the back and showed her tiny bum. Her mind was made up. She would become well because she would do the hard work. Her skin was pale, but the spark in her eyes was back. She would be feeling better in no time.

Chain-Breaking Freedom: Christy Rodriguez's Gutsy Girl Story

I met Christy Rodriguez a few years ago and instantly connected with her. It's impossible to not like her. Christy has a zeal for life and a passion for Christ that inspires me. Christy is an extrovert if I've ever met one; she's the life of the party with a serious case of FOMO (fear of missing out). Christy is the director and CEO at Brave Girl Community and has a powerful testimony and ministry. Christy has battled several strongholds in life, ranging from chocolate, cheese dip, and Sonic vanilla cokes, to more spiritually debilitating strongholds such as alcoholism, smoking, adultery, and same-sex attraction. Christy is amazed at how far she has come in ten years, and so am I. I'm honored to share her story in the pages of this book.

A Cry for Help—and God's Amazing Answer

"God, help me! Why can't I stop? I don't want to die, but I don't want to live, either." I said this prayer on a morning much like many others. Awaking with a massive hangover, I got up to see if my Jeep was in the garage. Thank God, it was. I didn't remember driving home, or anything past 9 p.m. from the night before. I had escaped harm/death from drinking and driving once again. This had become the norm, and I knew that one day my norm would destroy me or someone else. But I couldn't stop. I walked into my bedroom and fell to my knees. I cried in desperation unlike ever before, "God, help me! Why can't I stop? I don't want to die, but I don't want to live, either." I felt trapped. Enslaved in so much bondage, I had opened doors that I just couldn't shut on my own anymore. How did I get here? How had I gotten to this point?

Growing up, I was a happy blond-haired, blue-eyed twelve-year-old girl who wanted to be a teacher and a coach. You could always find me outside playing sports with the boys, riding my bike, kissing someone's puppy, or laughing and joking with my friends. I went to college on a soccer scholarship, was president of my sorority, graduated cum laude, and had the job I wanted including my dream car, a JEEP! But it still wasn't enough, and I couldn't understand why.

As I searched for fulfillment in everything but God, I drifted further from God, into alcoholism and eventually into my lesbian identity, my "true self." Edging God out of my life had created this self-centered mindset that helped me gather up quite a collection of pride, fears, resentments, poor decisions, lies, shame, guilt, unhealthy co-dependent relationships, and a whole lot of alcohol and cigarettes. My collection bag had become so full that I couldn't carry it another day.

At twenty-eight years old, I was finally at the end of myself, which would ironically be the beginning of my "true self," the one God created me to be. It began on my knees. The morning I said that prayer above was the beginning of my walk into freedom. And although I wasn't convinced God was even listening, I gave Him a chance anyway.

It was a simple, sincere act of faith, of humble surrender. That prayer was the beginning of an honest, heart wrenching, coming face-to-face with myself journey that would change me forever. It would catapult me into love and understanding of Jesus Christ that I had never known. The journey was going to take work, though, and God knew I needed Jesus with skin on to walk alongside me. That's when Jackie entered my life. She was fifty-five and full of spunk, wisdom, and colorful red hair. She loved God and Janis Joplin and had a big heart for helping women get sober. She had experienced her bouts of addiction and knew exactly where I was coming from. She fed me taco soup, sat with me, prayed with me, and laughed with me. She walked me through my entire past while continually pointing me back to God's truth. She never judged me. She just loved me as I was and let God do His thing. And He did!

James 5:16 reads, "Confess your sins and pray for each other and . . . you may be healed."

I confessed every sin I could remember to Jackie, sins I just knew I would take to my grave. Some of them felt impossible to say but, somehow, they came out of my mouth. We went through my sexual past, my resentments, my fears, and all the ways I had harmed other people. After confessing my deepest secrets and pain, she looked at me and said, "You are a beautiful child of God and He loves you so much." Her words pierced me like I was hearing them for the first time, and the shame fell off as if someone walked up behind me and removed the most oppressive and thickest winter coat right off my back. I realized that despite my sin or anything I had ever thought, felt, done, said, or wanted to do, God loved me that day just the same as the day I was born. He had chosen me all along, even when I rejected Him. Freedom began to enter my life, and I began to experience God in a whole new way.

Christy Rodriguez

The freedom Christy experienced in her life is something you can experience, too. I love the way Christy described her freedom encounter as shame literally falling off her; the heaviness she had been carrying with her on a daily basis was gone. Only an encounter with Jesus can do that. I believe it can happen right where you are today. In whatever room you find yourself reading this book—shame falling off even while you are holding this book, with tears streaming down your lovely face. Chains are breaking, and Jesus is doing the heavy lifting to set you free.

Freedom! The Word Is Your Weapon

> But Scripture has locked up everything under the control of sin, so that what was promised, being given through faith in Jesus Christ, might be given to those who believe.
>
> Galatians 3:22

The enemy targets those things we are actively working on. He is not creative; his tricks are the same thing on repeat. Where the enemy tries to destroy you, the God who is on your side desires to employ you. You can move forward in confidence and stand on this promise:

> In him and through faith in him we may approach God with freedom and confidence.
>
> Ephesians 3:12

Truth Your Soul Needs

We can have freedom and confidence in Christ over our:

Insecurities

Fear

Mistakes, both in the past and in the future

We can trust God through our biggest transitions in life:

Jobs

Relocation

Marriage

We can rely on His constancy through our changing roles:

Motherhood
Friendships
Family

We can depend on the Lord's provision for our health:

Emotional
Mental
Physical

Reflective Questions

1. What battle is God training you for?
2. Who will you be if you continue to hide, if you stay stuck? Who will remain lost along with you?
3. What shame will fall off you when you are truly free?

Gutsy Prayer

Lord,

Your Word says that in you and through faith in you we may approach you with freedom and confidence (Ephesians 3:12). Help me to walk boldly in the confidence you have for me.

I believe that "I will walk about in freedom, for I have sought out your precepts" (Psalm 119:45). Help me today to seek your ways above my own.

I praise you, for out of my distress I called to you, and you answered me and set me free (Psalm 118:5). You are near to me and hear my requests.

In Jesus' name, amen.

10

Beyond the Breakthrough

On my way to church one summer evening while the sky still had enough sunlight, I drove down a gravel road near my house. I found myself slowing down to drink in the beauty and splendor of multicolored wild flowers growing in a field nearby. While the flowers bloom without worry or care, I watch the hearts of the women I love spin and labor until their beautiful heads hit the pillow. They live in the grind and unholy hustle, finding themselves hurried and tied up from worries. I found that our answer to "How are you?" had changed from "I'm fine" to "I'm tired." Instead of blooming, we are withered and haggard. I feel the tug of it, too, the chronic nag of worry and things that do not add to my day—they simply deplete me of the beautiful things I could enjoy instead of focusing on more things to worry about. Somehow, we all find ourselves wrecked and wondering how we got there in the first place. But I prayed this night would be different for the group of women I was leading.

It didn't take long for the conversation to flow and the masks to be torn off. Tears made tracks down pretty faces, and I wondered if they knew how beautiful being messy really is. We wiped the salty desperation from our faces, unashamed that we came thirsty and needy. Every face told a story— most of them the same, just in different seasons. I'm tired of watching the shame bully throw guilt in the faces of godly girls just doing their best. I didn't expect them to open up right away. But I knew this to be a universal truth: If I hold back, so will they.

Somehow lost in translation, this thing of showing up to church and serving became a noose around a few necks. And as much as I hate to even type this . . . they love Jesus but had stopped loving the church. Maybe it's because I'm forty-two, or maybe it's because I know what it's like to be shamed into service. Perhaps it's because I have served in just about every capacity in the church that I wholeheartedly reject the shaming approach to servanthood. Not because I don't love working in different roles, but because I do love serving in the right roles.

One hour can change everything, and sometimes just showing up needs to be enough.

Words flowed from an unscripted plan, and I knew that was when God did His best work in me. No list or perfect outline. No desire to edit out the ugly side of the wrestle of womanhood. Just an intimate group of women showing up wrecked and hearing words that remove the shame-noose of perfection around heads trying to stay above water. Perfectionism is fear-based hiding, so what are you afraid that people will see? Author Holley Gerth explains:

> The pursuit of perfection can keep us from discovering God's purpose for our lives. It can distort who he created us to be, and then the world misses out on the gifts only we have to offer.[1]

That night I saw freedom stirring in the hearts of women ready for real change that lasts. Some said nothing, and some dove headfirst into the deep and gave us the gift of flawed beauty by saying, "I'm starving here." I thought about the woman pleading for her daughter. I thought about how most of the time we are so slow to ask for help for ourselves. But when it comes to our children or our loved ones, we lay down our pride and the shame of being needy for the hope of something in the supernatural. I recalled the exchange of words between a gutsy woman and Jesus, and the disciples who thought she was a nuisance and wanted to dismiss her.

Coming to Jesus needy and empty-handed was the catalyst for her miracle.

> And Jesus went away from there and withdrew to the district of Tyre and Sidon. And behold, a Canaanite woman from that region came out and was crying, "Have mercy on me, O Lord, Son of David; my daughter is severely oppressed by a demon." But he did not answer her a word. And his disciples came and begged him, saying, "Send her away, for she is crying out after us." He answered, "I was sent only to the lost sheep of the house of Israel." But she came and knelt before him, saying, "Lord, help me." And he answered, "It is not right to take the children's bread and throw it to the dogs." She said, "Yes, Lord, yet even the dogs eat the crumbs that fall from their masters' table." Then Jesus answered her, "O woman, great is your faith! Be it done for you as you desire." And her daughter was healed instantly.
>
> Matthew 15:21–28 ESV

We are so desperate for something real that we will take the crumbs falling from another woman's table because we don't think we are worthy of a full meal and unleashed blessings from

God. Shame and perfectionism have become our kryptonite, and coming to church admitting that we are needy has become ridiculously taboo. Our messiness is often the precursor for the miraculous. We are so afraid of our small offerings. Yet in this case, a needy woman ready for crumbs was more than enough to stop Jesus in His tracks to praise her faith and grant her desire. He even had time to give the disciples a verbal spanking and a lesson on what reaching lost sheep looks like. It doesn't look like perfection or shame at all; it looks like praise and a soul-satisfied, spirit-fed faith. You don't have to hide. You don't have to be perfect. You don't have to dismiss your small and messy life, because God can use it all for His glory.

Worry, the Nagging Voice Inside

I spent a majority of my life worrying about everything and nothing, constantly in knots trying to mentally prepare myself for the worst in every situation. Whether there *was* really a situation to be concerned about or not, I could come up with something to waste my time. I tried to make myself feel better by saying it was just my way of being prepared for the unknown, but what I was really doing was waging war against myself. I come from a long line of worriers; each of them means well and wants nothing but the best for others. But I found myself on the other side of anxiety with a question from the Word of God that put me in my place: What good was I doing by worrying? How could I call it nurturing and compassion when it was unsettling the deepest places within me?

A mentor of mine once told me that no one could take better care of me than I could. After a few health scares, I learned the hard way that pushing myself too hard ended badly more often than not. I had to learn how to practice self-care, which sounds like a load of horse poo to people who are lower maintenance, but you try cleaning warm manure off your shoe and tell me how low-maintenance that is for you. Sometimes it's better to look where you're going, assess all your needs, and take care of yourself accordingly. You can tend to your heart without being worried or stressed.

> Can any one of you by worrying add a single hour to your life?
>
> And why do you worry about clothes? See how the flowers of the field grow. They do not labor or spin. Yet I tell you that not even Solomon in all his splendor was dressed like one of these. If that is how God clothes the grass of the field, which is here today and tomorrow is thrown into the fire, will he not much more clothe you—you of little faith? So do not worry, saying, "What shall we eat?" or "What shall we drink?" or "What shall we wear?" For the pagans run after all these things, and your heavenly Father knows that you need them. But seek first his kingdom and his righteousness, and all these things will be given to you as well. Therefore do not worry about tomorrow, for tomorrow will worry about itself. Each day has enough trouble of its own.
>
> Matthew 6:27–34

What if I told you that proving yourself and jumping through hoops would cause you to miss the most important reason why we long to give the best of who we are to God and the ones we love? As I began searching the pages in Scripture, I felt God leading me to dive deeper into the history of someone who was vastly misunderstood and underrated. I met her in the pages of Scripture with fresh eyes. This time I wanted to know her, not just read about her. Beyond labels and limitations, of which she had plenty, I saw a legacy of godliness and getting stuff done. I found myself writing her a letter after combing through pages, commentaries, and familiar passages because she is so much like us—a broken girl who found the One who makes us whole.

But here is how she is different from those of us who find ourselves still in need of mending: She let go of her past because her newfound purpose was stronger than the chains that used to tie her frail hands. Mary Magdalene lived beyond her breakthrough.

To the woman, question mark, and mystery named Mary Magdalene:

*People still talk about you, speculations mostly, saying you were young and beautiful and troubled. Only one seems true—the troubled part. They have tried to Hollywood-ify and glamorize you because a scandal appeals to them more than the truth. They have found a box to put you in much like the one they thought you held over your Savior's head, anointing Him with perfume and tears and gratitude. It could have been you. It could have been all of us—**grateful girls motivated by love, feeling much like we owe our most priceless, box-sized gift. We are still carrying small boxes, thinking that is all we are worth.** Somehow still shattering that box of gratitude fueled by grace and hustling until we are exhausted from trying to earn what is already ours. It seems to me that God is shattering the box we've been putting ourselves in. If we will read His Word and believe, that all of those promises are for us, not just the unlabeled, mostly together people. Even the "mostly together" ones still feel the walls closing in, boxed and remaining very small because unboxed women are a threat to the enemy of our souls. They even make the churchy people nervous.*

Trust me, I have cardboard cuts from ripping open my box. The unboxed are the prayerful ones who pray until something happens, work until their hands ache, and love even the ones who are so stinking hard to love. They keep going because quitting is out of the equation. After searching the Scriptures while trying to figure you out, I believe I have found all that I really need to know about your story. You were set free to serve and to be not only faithful, but fruitful and powerfully effective. ***Your grateful soul was what motivated you to service. You were too busy pleasing God to concern yourself with pleasing others. You served the One who set you free, not the box that was way too small for you.***

Being freed from seven demons, you left little time for speculation because you were too busy getting stuff done. Your hustle was different from mine. You see, at times I'm still trying to prove myself. But that is only making me tired. So I give up. Gratefulness will be my motivation, too, because I've been freed from far more than seven things.

Anxiety
Depression
Infertility
Fear
Insecurity
People pleasing
Proving myself
Working to earn love and measure up

I've been freed from saying nothing because I want so much to be nice; now I can say what I must and hold my own with a brand-new backbone. I can take criticism, sift it like sand, and remove the shards of what is simply not true. I can take the criticism from others who are fruitful and faithful like you because they love me and have established a relationship with me. I can do so many things now because I have been set free from so many things, just like you. I learned how to shut down as a child through childhood trauma, yet becoming free in Christ propelled me to figure out how to come back alive again instead of being pleasing and invisible. I learned how to be who God wanted me to be, and to love the woman I have become.

Seven demons couldn't thwart the power of Jesus, who needed you as a member of His support team. You assisted Jesus in ministry; your face was woven into key moments: the cross, death, and resurrection. You were a witness to the crucifixion, present at His burial; you were faithful in the hard and heartbreaking things. You kept company with older women, so either they were your peers and close in age, or you were smart enough to surround yourself with mentors, sisters, and spiritual mamas who were fruitful and faithful—not busybodies, but busy with holy work. So maybe you weren't young. Age aside, you were wise.

You stood outside by the tomb weeping, and two angels asked you a question: "Woman, why are you weeping?"

You answered, "Because they have taken away my Lord, and I do not know where they have laid Him" (see John 20:13).

Jesus showed himself to you, called you **woman** *and then by name. You were there when everyone else had left. You ran back to tell the other disciples, and they didn't believe you (Mark 16:10). I mean, after all, you were still referred to as the woman with seven demons cast out. You* *probably didn't mind, since they didn't believe the other two after you, either (Mark 16:13).*

You wept because Jesus was **yours**. *Not once do I see you limited by your weakness, not as a woman or by your tattered past. You were seeking Him and serving Him; that was your fuel—not proving yourself. I want to be like you. Grateful. Grace-filled. Too busy to be boxed. Too busy to look back. Fruitfully faithful. At the intersection where labels meet legacy, I'll take the long road of servitude serving my Lord. My teacher. My God who is much too big for a box. And my Savior who made me much too big for one, as well.*

Today I ditch the box because of an empty tomb. Pursuing God and serving Him out of a heart filled with gratitude is our fuel. Loving Him with all of our heart and soul is our focus. Whispers and stares couldn't hold Mary Magdalene back. They can't hold us back, either. In a culture that told her to go to the back of the line, if for no other reason than because of her womanhood, she was mentioned fourteen times in the gospels. In eight of those references she is mentioned with other women, but she always is at the top of the list, which means that she was a leader in service and held a prestigious place.

I'm barely scratching the surface of what all we can glean learning about Mary Magdalene. You have no idea how desperately I needed to study her this past week. I ran my fingers through pages, looked at commentaries, and cried the kind of tears that sting a little from working so hard and realizing that I didn't have to prove myself anymore. My gratitude can propel me to service, not to seek the approval of others. What I feel right now is the joy of fruitfulness and favor—and that makes me pretty happy. This is what it feels like to live beyond breakthrough and walk in freedom. We figure out the hard things. We search the Scriptures for the answers we need. We cry and release those things and find the healing we need every time. This is living beyond the breakthrough, kicking worry in the face, and deciding that we will be about our Father's business and not worry about those who are hard to please. This is real freedom.

The Small

People, even good ones, will discredit what you have to offer. We could fault them for it, but they do the same thing to themselves. One boy with one lunch and five thousand hungry mouths to feed. Phillip, a man of God and disciple, looked at his pocket change and called it not enough and insufficient. Then he looked at the boy's lunch—five barley loaves and two fishes—and he called it not enough: "What are they among so many?"

But the boy gave it all as a willing offering. What we have never looks like much. The small things we hold in our hands, the ways we dismiss God's greater plan because we are running on empty, shorthanded, and often shortchanged. Carrying around our pocket full of small, limited by our belief that we are living in a place of not enough. We size up our offering, even cast it aside or dismiss it altogether. But not our Jesus. He takes small and multiplies it. He takes lack and turns it into abundance. He gave thanks for the broken bread that would feed hungry hearts. Later they gathered up the fragments of "more than enough" so that nothing was lost.

Small is where God shows up and becomes the more we long for.

The widow with her small cakes and a son and a hungry prophet. The wedding party who had just run out of wine. They saw the lack, and they felt it, just like we do. We see the impossible and declare it a disaster and disappointment. But God sees something far beyond our lack and meets our needs. Sometimes not in the way we choose, but always in the way we need. It's not lacking at all; it's the dance floor at the best party ever thrown. It's not just a brown paper sack with a cold lunch; it's a feast that satisfies thousands, with loads of leftovers.

Jesus took the loaves of bread and multiplied them. From one person's small offering, a multitude was fed and even more was left over. God is in the "not enough" business, and He wants to do the same thing with you. Don't look at empty pockets and empty hands; reach out with eager hands in faith, trusting God that they will be filled and will be useful. He is not the God of empty promises; He is a God who delivers. He is more than enough, and He wants what you have to offer.

Truth Your Soul Needs

Jesus is good at taking broken things and not enough to nurture needy hearts. Most of the time, He asks the one running on empty for their greatest sacrifice of obedience, knowing that will be the most sustaining, life-giving miracle—to give yourself away. The gift of giving it all while doubting that it's enough. We all feel the heaviness that comes from smallness, but God stretches our small and reminds us that His faithfulness never runs out.

Living beyond your breakthrough is showing up with whatever you have to offer and knowing that God can and will use it.

Reflective Questions

1. Can you identify with Mary Magdalene? From what has Jesus set you free?

2. Which demons are still dogging you? They are no match for our Lord! "But Scripture has locked up everything under the control of sin, so that what was promised, being given through faith in Jesus Christ, might be given to those who believe" (Galatians 3:22).
3. What are your small things that God can make much of if you offer them to Him?

Gutsy Prayer

Lord,

You are more than enough, even when I am running on empty. When I am hard-pressed, I can cry out to you, and you will bring me into a spacious place (Psalm 118:5). You are bigger than any box that I can place you in. My feeling of lack, or not enough, could never stop or hinder your faithfulness to me. I'm ready to give you everything I have to offer and live beyond breakthrough to walk in true freedom. You have come so that I have life and have it more abundantly (John 10:10). You are the more than my soul longs for. Help me to be set free to be faithfully fruitful like Mary Magdalene.

In Jesus' name, amen.

PART 2

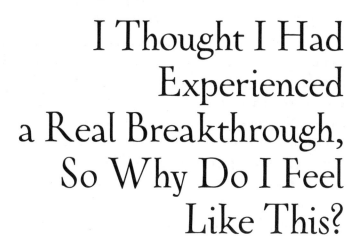

I Thought I Had Experienced a Real Breakthrough, So Why Do I Feel Like This?

I NEED TO TALK TO YOU about something you don't want to hear, but first I need you to simmer down for a second and listen while you feel like you are making progress. I am not only your overly perky yet equally snarky Breakthrough Coach, I am also the Queen of Crash and Burn. You know how I talk about the excruciating pain right before your breakthrough? It's because I lived it so many times and would cycle back into old habits, until one crisis when I realized how whole and healed I truly was because my new normal was victory, not just setbacks. I was different because I looked at everything that happened, whether good or bad, with a heart that trusted God fully, not just when everything was going my way.

After you experience those birthing pains that have you pleading for something strong (or possibly illegal) to numb the pain, comes a moment when the thrill kicks in and you hold something precious close to your chest, promising to never let that feeling slip away ever again. You are holding your promise. You have climbed the Everest of your emotional stuckness and danced on that mountain with bursting lungs. And then you realize that no one lives on Breakthrough Mountain forever. You, sweet warrior, have to climb down. Maybe you don't believe me now. None of us want the Jesus high to end, but it does. We want to have the head-over-heels-in-love feeling forever, whether that is in our marriage, motherhood, or our Christian walk. We love the excitement of newness, but there comes a profound moment when we learn to root ourselves deeply in Christ whether we are feeling it or not. We become believers who have made a commitment to Christ to stick it out. You are in this for the long haul, and there are blessings for your faithfulness that far outweigh the temporary Jesus high and adrenaline rush.

When you merge back into the mundane and messy moments of ordinary life, you will, as I have, feel a sadness in a corner of your soul and wonder, *Is this it?* I need you to put this on your radar now and make a pact with me that you will reread this chapter when you start to feel the butterflies leave the pit of your stomach and something slightly sour take their place. There is nothing on earth worse than a sour Christian who smells like bitterness every time she walks into a room. I have been her, and I don't like her much. We have all been Debbie Downer and taken what would have been a pleasant discussion and flushed it down the toilet with our negativity. It's not pretty, is it?

So what do you do when you've been disappointed with what your reality looks like? How do you stomach the ache you feel inside while trying to make sense of it all? What do you do then? You freaking get back to work and fight beyond what you feel. This will not be how your story ends; it will not even be your droopy middle. Nuh-uh. I will not tell you to fake it till you make it or something else cheesy, like faith-it till you make it. I'm completely fine with you throwing a conniption. I certainly throw one from time to time; most ticked-off Southern girls do. I have hard evidence against a mighty man of God and prophet who threw a fit, of sorts, right after a major victory and answer to prayer. Before I move on to the big fit, it's important to highlight that before Elijah received a death threat, there was a significant drought that lasted for nearly three years. That is a long time to go without rain, especially when everything depended on it. The people demanded to know who controlled the rain—the Lord God of Israel or Baal? A showdown occurred to prove who would hear the cries of the people. The prophets of Baal cried and cut themselves until blood gushed, but there was no answer; no voice could be heard, and no one paid attention (1 Kings 18:28–29). They made quite a scene, to no avail. Then Elijah did his thing.

> And it came to pass, *at the time* of the offering of the *evening* sacrifice, that Elijah the prophet came near and said, "Lord God of Abraham, Isaac, and Israel, let it be known this day that You *are* God in Israel and I *am* Your servant, and that I have done all these things at Your word. Hear me, O Lord, hear me, that this people may know that You *are* the Lord God, and that You have turned their hearts back *to You* again."

> Then the fire of the Lord fell and consumed the burnt sacrifice, and the wood and the stones and the dust, and it licked up the water that *was* in the trench. Now when all the people saw it, they fell on their faces; and they said, "The Lord, He *is* God! The Lord, He *is* God!"
>
> And Elijah said to them, "Seize the prophets of Baal! Do not let one of them escape!" So they seized them; and Elijah brought them down to the Brook Kishon and executed them there.
>
> Then Elijah said to Ahab, "Go up, eat and drink; for *there is* the sound of abundance of rain." So Ahab went up to eat and drink. And Elijah went up to the top of Carmel; then he bowed down on the ground, and put his face between his knees, and said to his servant, "Go up now, look toward the sea."
>
> So he went up and looked, and said, "*There is* nothing." And seven times he said, "Go again."
>
> Then it came to pass the *seventh time*, that he said, "There is a cloud, as small as a man's hand, rising out of the sea!" So he said, "Go up, say to Ahab, 'Prepare *your chariot*, and go down before the rain stops you.'"
>
> 1 Kings 18:36–44 NKJV, emphasis added

Elijah believed his prayer was answered before the answer came. He believed his miracle was on the way and that it was important for all of them to look for it. Elijah was praying persistently, seven times! What would have happened if he had stopped after prayer five or six? No matter what we face in life, when we have a promise of provision from God, we cannot stop praying until our prayers are answered.

Even after victory that looked like raindrops falling from the sky, and despite God proving himself faithful and mighty, Elijah still had a crisis of faith when he received a death threat. Everyone has moments of humanity, Old Testament prophets included. After Elijah's multiple victories, including the one on

Mount Carmel against the prophets of Baal, and another that was a persistent prayer to end the drought, a death threat was made by the hag Jezebel, and it was enough to make Elijah run for his life. He picked up his skirt—okay, his robe—and ran for the hills. Why? Because women are scary, especially when they are trying to silence the voice of truth by killing prophets. Elijah was the last man standing (1 Kings 18:45–19:21).

> But he himself went a day's journey into the wilderness, and came and sat down under a broom tree. And he prayed that he might die, and said, "It is enough! Now, Lord, take my life, for I am no better than my fathers!"
>
> Then as he lay and slept under a broom tree, suddenly an angel touched him, and said to him, "Arise and eat." Then he looked and there by his head was a cake baked on coals, and a jar of water. So he ate and drank, and lay down again. And then the angel of the Lord came back the second time, and touched him, and said, "Arise and eat, because the journey is too great for you." So he arose, and ate and drank; and he went in the strength of that food for forty days and forty nights as far as Horeb, the mountain of God.
>
> 1 Kings 19:4–8 NKJV

What I love about this story is that it confirms what I believe to be true: A good nap and meal can cure just about anything and help our perspective. It wasn't that the threat facing him wasn't real, because it was. I believe the fear that seized Elijah was meant to be felt and faced. I also believe that when he felt this kind of fear, his relationship with God was solid enough that he could be honest and raw with his emotions. The angel of the Lord came to Elijah multiple times and told him to do two things: to get up and to eat something. Elijah had a long journey ahead of him and was told that the journey is "too much for you." But it wasn't too much for Elijah after he did nothing but sleep and eat some snacks delivered to him by an angel. The journey was too much for him, but not if he took that time to receive sustenance, to simply stop, rest, and be replenished. Elijah still had to make the journey, still had work to do. And something else I love about this story is that throughout his journey, the Lord asked him what he was going to do: "What are you doing here, Elijah?" (1 Kings 19:9).

There is a partnership between us and the God we serve. We are a team and we do things together; He leads and we do our best to obey and follow His leading. Hard things will come our way. Our journey will be too much for us to complete in our own strength, but it will never be too much for our God. Never.

We can trust God, who revealed himself to Elijah in a powerful way:

> Then He said, "Go out, and stand on the mountain before the Lord." And behold, the Lord passed by, and a great and strong wind tore into the mountains and broke the rocks in pieces before the Lord, *but* the Lord *was* not in the wind; and after the wind an earthquake, *but* the Lord *was* not in the earthquake; and after the earthquake a fire, *but* the Lord *was* not in the fire; and after the fire a still small voice.
>
> 1 Kings 19:11–12 NKJV, emphasis added

God was not in the wind, earthquake, or fire. God was the still, small voice. We can trust God that through wind and fire, or whatever comes our way, He will be that still, small voice that stirs up courage in our hearts to keep going. After we throw our fits, and liquid question marks roll down our cheeks, God will still be God, and He will still be for us. We have that assurance of soul that He will never leave or forsake us or grow weary of our questions. Take a nap, eat a snack, and go fight the battles with your name on them. And be certain that you have already won the minute you get knocked down and decide to get back up again. Get up, warrior, get up. God has this.

Soul Strategy When We Aren't Feeling It:

I will pray until the answer comes.
I will believe that the answer is on the way.
I will listen to the still, small voice.
I will partner with God to fight my battles.
I will, no matter what, keep going.

11

Abundantly More, Ending Our Tug-of-War with Joy

I HAVE NEVER HEARD ANYONE explain our tug-of-war with joy like Dr. Brené Brown does. She calls it "foreboding joy."[1] Joy shows up with an unwelcome guest tagging along. So instead of feeling happiness, lingering sadness rushes in because joy brings the vulnerability of losing it all at a moment's notice. "Our actual experiences of joy—those intense feelings of deep spiritual connection and pleasure—seize us in a very vulnerable way," Brown writes.[2] "When something good happens, our immediate thought is that we'd better not let ourselves truly feel it, because if we really love something we could lose it. So we shut down our ability to completely enjoy so that we can also shut down our capacity for feeling loss."

"Joy is the most vulnerable emotion we experience," Brown says. "And if you cannot tolerate joy, what you do is you start dress-rehearsing tragedy."[3]

In the past I have been the girl dress-rehearsing tragedy, almost uncertain of how to handle the joy and freedom I was walking on a daily basis. Instead of embracing it and praising God for it, I was looking for things to worry about. How could someone long for joy, yet fear it at the same time? I couldn't blame it on the enemy of my soul because I was the guilty party looking to sabotage and destroy the new strength and constant in my life: joy. In Brown's extensive research, she has met people with a profound capacity for joy. The difference, she says, is that when something really blissful happened to them, they felt grateful. "Instead of using it as a warning to start practicing disaster, they used it as a reminder to practice gratitude," Brown says.[4]

My friend Keri was the first one to tell me about foreboding joy after she listened to Brown's interview with Oprah. I watched the video alone, several times, taking notes and pausing to really process this information on a level where I could grow in this area and understand how we as believers can complicate God's greatest blessings because of our fear. Keri and I have spent years talking about how this is truly a struggle for her, and for all of us who have walked through tragedy in life. It's become an ongoing mission for us to see the ways that we sabotage our personal happiness. Today, Keri and I met a friend for lunch. What was supposed to be an hour-long meal turned into over two hours because that's what friends do when we are catching up and checking in on how people are *really* doing. Surface doesn't cut it—only depth and honest conversation will tell us everything we need to know.

Keri has been the queen of foreboding joy and the first one to admit it, but never so much in her life as when she found herself falling in love in her forties after a heartbreaking divorce seven years prior. Of all the good and precious gifts I have wanted for my friend, having someone who treasured her as the precious prize she is has been at the top of my list. The reason I admire Keri so much is because she turns to Jesus and isn't afraid to do the hard work it takes to set her heart free. No one I know will confront every single lingering stronghold in her life like Keri does. She is the reason I have done the same thing for myself, because nothing should ever stand in the way of our healing and freedom—especially not us!

As Keri and I walked out of the restaurant, I brought up the *one* thing that never came up in our conversation over a two-hour lunch: her love life. As I asked about her heart and the way she was feeling now that marriage was being discussed seriously, foreboding joy entered our conversation. Because she is the deepest thinker you will ever meet, wrestling and overthinking everything is part of who she is. I dare not question the aspect that makes her uniquely Keri, which causes her to examine every angle and layer of her past, her right now, and her future. I trust her process because I have found her to be a woman after the heart of God above all other things, especially when it comes to pursuits of the heart.

I ran through a mental checklist out loud. Red flags? None. Knowing someone through all four seasons and long enough to *really* know a person? Check. Character issues? Passed with flying colors. Pursues the heart of the girl I admire and treasures her the way Christ loves and cares for the church? Nailing it daily and consistently. Hallelujah. Sees her ministry and is proud of the woman she is instead of threatened by her enormous success in life? Wholeheartedly, in every way it matters most. So what's the real problem? It could only be fear.

I lean in and say something that takes even me by surprise. "Maybe you need to learn how to enjoy walking in abundance instead of waiting for the other shoe to drop? Abundance is your new norm." Keri looks at me with wide eyes. She just got spanked with the truth, and she knows it. She smiles and tells me good-bye, and then jumps in her car and writes down what I just said to her. The truth for all of us walking beyond our breakthrough is the promise that there is an abundance of joy that we dare not sabotage.

> The thief does not come except to steal, and to kill, and to destroy. I have come that they might have life, and they might have it more abundantly.
>
> John 10:10 NKJV

Abundantly: **abounding fullness of joy and strength for mind, body, and soul.** An abundant life is not about what we have, how much money we make, two-point-five kids, and a house pet living in your dream home. Abundance is a state of the heart. Our only constant when life is constantly changing is that we serve a God who is faithful and cannot be anything other than faithful. He came that we may have life, but not just any life—He offers us a life filled with abundance of soul and joy that can fill us up and sustain us despite whatever we are facing. We don't have to dress-rehearse for tragedy; we can embrace our joy with gratitude. And by doing so, we increase our capacity for an overflowing, unstoppable joy that cannot be stolen from us.

Soul Prosperity

Women like you are my heroes, and my life is enriched because friends have taken down their walls with me and have let me see the struggle they are engaged in on a daily basis. You are the freedom speakers and truth tellers. You are the warm hugs when the world is giving someone a swift kick in the pants. You are the trailblazers paving the way for your daughters and granddaughters to live in the fullness of God because you are living it as the most beautiful example right in front of them.

I know that at times you feel like what you do to serve your family and others goes unnoticed, but the One who matters most sees it. When you fix a meal and take it to a sick neighbor, no one is going to feature your sacrifice of time on the nightly news, but you are doing the most important holy work of showing up for others. No one is going to throw a parade in your honor because you've done the dishes for the third time and cleaned up after your messy kids, but you are doing the most important, holy work.

What would happen if you woke up and knew for certain that everything you did that day that was incredibly boring and mundane was a bigger deal than you make of it? In your mind, you are doing what simply needs to be done. But what if I told you that your faithfulness in the little things is what will make the greatest impact in the long run? You are proving you are another one of God's warriors that He can trust with the small things and the big things. Inside your heart is a dream you are afraid to dream, but I hope you can see that breakthrough is all about dreaming those dreams while you are wide awake. It's taking what you have learned in those hidden seasons of feeling so small to make a wake of influence in the women and your community around you.

You don't need your name in lights or in a book to be the greatest influencer in your corner of the world. We simply need you to be living beyond your breakthrough and sharing your stories to offer hope to the ones who find themselves in the trenches now, begging God for their inner war to end. Before the gunpowder dissipates, they need to see your steady presence in the haze. You will be the one who brings clarity as the dust settles in their life. You will bandage wounds and pour in the healing salve that softens the sting with kindness. You don't have to tell them how to handle their battle, you can just tell them how God helped you handle yours and that they can trust Him with theirs, too. You are not just a survivor of your broken battle, you are a warrior who has done the hard work of pursuing freedom. Still unsure of what you have to offer? Start there.

> The one who is faithful in a very little is also faithful in much, and the one who is dishonest in a very little is also dishonest in much.
>
> Luke 16:10 NET

> See, I am doing a new thing! Now it springs up; do you not perceive it? I am making a way in the wilderness and streams in the wasteland.
>
> Isaiah 43:19

Sister, you are the new thing. You are the light that shows the way in the wilderness. Your soul is the stream that refreshes those around you. Your laugh is the one that fills up the room and reminds others of the joy they are missing. You are the new thing—the beautiful new thing—and that, my friend, is what this world is waiting on. Cling to the fire in your soul with everything you have and make a promise to your sweet self that you will not coast through life, that you will dare to live with faith when the world around you seems to be on autopilot.

> Beloved, I pray that you may prosper in all things and be in health, just as your soul prospers. For I rejoiced greatly when brethren came and testified of the truth that is in you, just as you walk in truth. I have no greater joy than to hear that my children walk in truth.
>
> 3 John 2–4 NKJV

Stay in the Moment

Our schedule was rushed last Christmas Eve because it happened to be a Sunday. Sunday is different for us, as ministers, because it's our biggest work day. It's ministry life, and as much as I have tried hard to balance life so my girls will love Jesus and love the church, there are times when I fail miserably and end up short-tempered due to the pressure I feel.

When we finally arrived at our family Christmas, I was feeling stressed and afraid that everyone would be upset with us. I dropped off my dog and my husband (and his bad back) at my parents' house to allow for more time with my dad's side of the family. That would make them happier, or at least more comfortable. After all, it's just like me to make sure everyone is happy—or at least happy-ish. Jonathan could watch football and sit in a comfortable chair, and I would be with my family. *Winning.* When it was just the three of us girls, I explained to my daughters that I would relax, and we would just get there when we got there. I told them I wanted them to love Christmas and love our family time. I knew that if I became frazzled I could ruin all of it, and that's the last thing I wanted to do.

Thankfully, no one was upset with us because we were running behind and an hour late. They were just glad we came. *We were so glad we were there.* My dad's side of the family is special to me, and being with them makes me feel closer to my grandma and my dad. Sure, it also makes me sad that they're not there, but I feel better knowing I'm with my family with the same shade of brown eyes as mine.

After everything was over and I was walking things out to my car, my Elise stopped me and asked for a hug. *I love hugs. I will always break for hugs.* I squeezed her tightly and we whispered, "I love you."

As I began to let go of my tiny teenager, standing on the small-town sidewalk with icy-cold air pressing in around us, I could feel myself switch to rush mode again. Rush home to be with my mom, husband, and dog. *Rush. Rush. Rush.*

Elise held me tighter, refusing to let go, and said, "Stay in the moment, Mom."

She said it twice. *Twice.*

"Stay in the moment."

Everything else could wait. I didn't have any fires to put out, nothing to clean up—just off to the next place. I squeezed her tighter. I relaxed as her tiny frame melted into mine. I didn't feel cold anymore or rushed. I felt peace. I felt steady. I wasn't sad anymore about missing my loved ones in heaven. I was loving the one in front of me well.

"Oh, baby, I will stay in the moment, because there is nothing that I love more than this. Nothing is more important than you and me together," I said.

What thirteen-year-old can tell you what they are missing from you? Mine did.

She wanted me all in, there in body and heart. She wanted me to stay in the moment, whatever it was or looked like, and feeling all of it instead of rushing off to the next one. She wanted me.

And I wanted to be wanted. Confession: I'm not doing everything right. I rarely do. But I try, and that's enough for me. I'm trying so hard to keep up and keep everyone happy, which is my jam, but usually that means I'm last on my list—and unfortunately means I'm the last on *other* lists as well, which creates more tension at times.

I have stayed in the moment, even when it's a frustrated one. That's super fun and super hard.

If I'm honest, I will tell you that being fully present is work, especially when you are "easier to deal with when you are nicer."

But a real breakthrough in your life means you know that you are worth it, even when you are less than perfect and might be ticked off . . . or harder to deal with. *Whatever.*

Say you're sorry. I've said it multiple times to my girls. The funny thing is, they get it because they get me and they love me anyway, because they know they are the most important thing in my world. I prove that by the life I give them year after year. They will always be the most important thing in my little world. More important than writing books and doing ministry. They *are* my ministry.

That is the first Christmas in years that I felt awake. And the first Christmas that I've had the energy to make Christmas merry because I'm feeling better than ever after having genetic testing for my depression and anxiety. Being on the *right* medication for three months has really shown me a few things, like how life can be more than simply checking off the days and trying to remember everything. For three years I was living and surviving, but I wasn't thriving. I was coping, and that's okay. But what's strange and wonderful and a tiny bit sad is all the Christmases I barely remember because I was in a fog of depression. Seasonal depression is horrible for me, but not this year. All the praise goes to Jesus for this healing, and I'm grateful for a doctor who told me I was worth it and that there were too many options for me to just "manage" my depression and get by.

Now I'm awake. I'm present. And I'm worth it. My people are worth it.

I'm also ready to break up with doing things the same way—simply checking off all the boxes on my to-do list. To be present means removing some of my boxes because I chose to be awake, to be present. And to know that my mental health and my well-being needs fewer boxes and needs my significant others to be awake, too, and ready to hear me when I ask for help and admit that I'm not Wonder Woman (but I'm pretty darn close).

Soul Strategy for Staying in the Moment

- Figure out what moments are worth staying in and stay in them.
- Figure out what moments are worth fighting for and fight for them.
- Don't place blame; own your part of whatever makes the holidays, or life, harder for you. Figure out why you're sad, why you feel unheard. Maybe you're saying it wrong or asking for help in a way that your people don't understand.
- If history repeats itself, and it often does, what part of your future would you like to change? What is inside of you that needs to change? Or be surrendered at the feet of Jesus?
- Whatever you do, don't go numb; that's the easy way out. Stay awake. Stay in the moment.
- Stay present. Don't settle for anything less than awake, even when it hurts. Don't look to others and expect them to be your Jesus or fix you. Only Jesus satisfies. He is what you need.
- Be you. That's enough. I always tell people that what I lack in talent I make up for in passion. When I've lost my spark, I know something is wrong and that my health is suffering. Most of the time, it just means I'm exhausted to the core. So if you are tired, take a nap. Don't just complain about it; do something to fix it.

Jesus said, "Come to me, all you who are weary and burdened, and I will give you rest" (Matthew 11:28).

He gives us rest, not lists.

"Take my yoke upon you and learn from me, for I am gentle and humble in heart, and you will find rest for your souls" (v. 29).

He lightens our load as we spend time in His presence and listen, really listen to Him and what He tells us in His word. Throw away your list, if only for a day. Take care of your heart; you're the only one in charge of that. *Stay in the moment. Feel everything.*

Soul Strategy for Letting Go of Perfection

I'm not exactly sure when I released my death grip on perfection, but when I did, the floodgates of my heart opened and made room for better space. I was trying to be good at everything—and I mean *everything*. Yet I was missing the sweetest parts of who God designed me to be. I was spinning my wheels so fast thinking I was doing noble and godly things. And I was, but I wasn't doing the right things. I was chronically distracted and dissatisfied. Trying to be good at everything meant I wasn't really good at anything at all because my life was undone and unfinished. I realized I wasn't listening to God because I was too preoccupied by my fears and what-ifs. By trying so hard to please others, I drifted further from my God-given purpose.

You know those people you are trying so hard to please? They can't see the real you if you are too busy trying to be the perfect version of yourself. The messy, real you is pretty spectacular. That girl who messes up and laughs at herself? Be that girl; she's much easier to like.

I'm starting a new adventure in my life, and to be honest, I'm scared to death. I'm wondering if I'll feel "mom guilt" from working so hard and being gone more. I'm worried that I'll be too tired to flirt with my husband. I'm worried that my stress acne will never clear up and that I'll have to buy zit cream until I'm sixty-five. I'm worried that I'll be that annoying girl trying to be good at everything again and be miserable. But I can't focus on all the ways I could fall short during this season of transition. I only have two goals right now: show up and be faithful. That's it, and that's enough. I'm not going to be able to do it all, so I'm taking that off the table. I'm taking it one day at a time and figuring it out as I go. It's impossible to give in to worry when I am trusting God to wrap me up in strength. Putting on strength is a choice I make daily to chase away the fears and unrealistic expectations.

We don't have to be perfect; we just have to be available. When a woman wears strength, she perceives what she has to offer is good. God has given us such good things to work with, so maybe just showing up and being faithful is more than enough to start with.

> She girds herself with strength, and strengthens her arms.
> She perceives that her merchandise is good, and her lamp does not go out by night.
>
> Proverbs 31:17–18 NKJV

I chose to switch from survival mode to find myself sustained in Christ. Perfection is off the table. I am ready to listen. I need to slow down, rearrange my priorities, relax, and find a different pace that can still be fruitful and far more meaningful. How can we find peace when we are trying to keep up with a hurried pace and everything in our lives is overly cluttered? Today

I woke up and had to repent and ask God for a spiritual reset. I had to forgive myself, which is so much harder for me than extending forgiveness to others. Are you ready to switch from survival mode to finding your soul sustained in Christ? Me too. What do you need to take off your list? Unrealistic expectations? Fear of the future? Are you constantly beating yourself up but freely offering kindness to everyone else?

Some days are magical while others are just *meh*. With living beyond your breakthrough comes a stability of soul whether life is messy or mundane. I love the thrill of the moment and celebrating important milestones, but there is a letdown after every spiritual high. There's the steady climb to our personal mountaintop, but for some reason there seems to be a walk of shame down the mountainside afterward, even when we are aware—sometimes even days later—that something monumental took place in our life.

We are still in a perpetual state of searching for the next thing, and we miss the stillness that comes as a gift to us. I find myself rushing through life at breakneck speed. I lie to myself and call it "just one of those seasons," but it looks a lot like hustling. It's a universal truth that when we are in go-mode, we are desperate for results. *Please tell me that all of these spinning plates aren't just a disaster waiting to happen.* I imagine myself removing each spinning plate, holding it tightly, and whispering something like, "You were never meant to spin, love. You were destined for dining, for providing something that sustains, not to be spinning so fast that no one can figure out your rightful shape or that you even have a place at the table."

It's in the spinning that we forget what it means to savor and enjoy the gift we bring to the table. I don't want to live in a chronic state of hustle. I just don't. I question my calendar and look at all of those very important things and wonder how much time I am spending with God. In the name of serving Him, sometimes I feel distracted instead of close to His heart. Something has to stop spinning, and that has to be me. I don't love to hustle, but I'm good at it. I'm good at having my hands in everything and can multitask like nobody's business, but I have to remind myself daily to stay present in my right now instead of looking ahead. My people deserve the gift of presence in body and heart and most important, in my mind—where my thoughts often run wild and take me to a place of checking things off my crazy-long list. My list looks like a noose instead of a plan, so I guard my days and quiet my heart . . . or I'll be in need of another breakthrough that looks a lot like letting go.

Taming the Tyranny of Lists

We are not slaves to our lists. They are supposed to work for us, not the other way around.

You can't rush through life and expect to have a meaningful life because you have missed moments in the madness of checking things off your list.

You can't rush greatness, you nurture it.

Your soul is worth your pressing pause on a few things to really figure out how many of those things actually belong on your list at all.

You don't have to become the next Big Thing or a trendsetter, sweet one; you are already one in a million—a masterpiece unaware of the treasure that is entirely your own.

You don't have to live a life of spinning plates to find yourself a place at the table.

> For thus says the Lord God, the Holy One of Israel: "In returning and rest you will be saved; In quietness and confidence shall be your strength."
>
> Isaiah 30:15 NKJV

Name Your Spinning Plates

Your spinning plate could look like a bake sale for the PTA—serving in a role that isn't connected with your talents, so you serve out of obligation and dread every minute of it. Your spinning plates could be saying yes to everyone who needs something and putting yourself, your family, and your precious sanity on the back burner. A spinning plate is anything that doesn't fit in this season of your life. List yours here.

Which ones are necessary, as in tied to your home life or work?

Which ones can you remove for now, press pause, and add at a later time?

____

____

____

> "Come to me, all you who are weary and burdened, and I will give you rest. Take my yoke upon you and learn from me, for I am gentle and humble in heart, and you will find rest for your souls. For my yoke is easy and my burden is light."
>
> Matthew 11:28–30

Truth Your Soul Needs

Freedom isn't about what we produce or achieve but rather who we are becoming in Christ. While I will be the first to tell you that all the effort you spend on working and fighting for your breakthrough is worth it, you need to know that now is the time to stop trying to hustle to earn your worthiness. The enemy will always try to distract you when the Holy Spirit is guiding you. While the enemy whispers in your ear all the things you should be doing, the Word says you trade up with God every single time:

"Where the Spirit of the Lord is, there is freedom" (2 Corinthians 3:17).

"In this world you will have trouble. But take heart! I have overcome the world" (John 16:33).

"[The Lord's] power is made perfect in weakness" (2 Corinthians 12:9).

"Weeping may stay for the night, but rejoicing comes in the morning" (Psalm 30:5).

"Lean not on your own understanding; in all your ways submit to him, and he will make your paths straight" (Proverbs 3:5-6).

Reflective Questions

1. Do you embrace joy, or fear it? Do you dress-rehearse tragedy?
2. Is staying in the moment difficult for you?
3. Is *your list* the same as *God's list for you*? Can you rest in Him even when all the boxes aren't checked off your list?

Gutsy Prayer

Lord,

You say in your Word to come to you, all who are weary and burdened, and you will give us rest (Matthew 11:28). You give us rest, not more lists. Help me today as I cast all my anxiety and cares on you because you care for me (1 Peter 5:7). Thank you for your steadfast love that never ceases or runs out on me even when I'm worn out. Your mercies never come to an end (Lamentations 3:22).

In Jesus' name, amen.

12

Healing Sisterhood

MY MINISTRY took on different shapes when I met a broken girl like me who was also in the spotlight of public ministry. Over Mexican food and a three-hour lunch, we spilled every broken detail in our lives and skipped the safe, normal, get-to-know-you questions. We both began to heal together. Healing sisterhood is real and it's powerful.

Real growth was when I realized that, even after all these years, I was whole but had pushed the wrong people away—like my college friend who has loved me for twenty years—because I was afraid I would only disappoint them. The thought of that was too much for me to handle. What if I was an adult who couldn't follow through? That scared the mess out of me, so I invited the controlling people to have more influence in my life and tried to please them. Because that's way better, right? Nope. That's JACKED ALL THE WAY UP. But their voices were louder, and I let them drown out the right voices.

Keri and I met eight years ago. When she came to our church she was wounded and suffering from a severe case of "church burn," a scar or battle wound that happened inside the church. Whether it is from leadership or a friend in the congregation, when it happens in a place you feel should be safe, it hurts more. The last thing she wanted was to become friends with the perky pastor's wife. But as soon as she found out I was a mixture of sweet and snarky, she decided to give me a chance.

You don't crowd women with walls; all they need to know is that you are there and you're not going anywhere. But whatever you do, don't hover. I'm not sure how long it took, but one day Keri asked me to go to lunch with her. A lasting friendship formed that was all about healing community—two women in ministry laying it all out on the table and saying the thing we couldn't say to just anyone: I'm still broken.

I'm terrible at small talk; I make it really awkward, and my attention deficit gets the best of me. At times, I find it all terribly boring and get distracted by anything that sparkles. But if you want to talk old wounds or share the embarrassing story that still makes you red-faced, I'm your girl. If I have one opportunity to get to know you, I want to see behind the wall we naturally put up as women until we feel safe. I want to see the real you, even if it's messy. If that means outing myself as a hot mess, that's okay, too.

If you make a woman feel safe, you'll never have to beg her to share her heart with you. Keri and I instantly found common threads in our stories: the results of divorce and sharing holidays, family addiction, and wreckage from angry, misspoken words. We both have suffered from verbal abuse and know how those words tend to be an echo in the mind. But in the middle of moments that could have wounded us the most, two broken girls fell in love with Jesus and kicked the statistics stacked against us in the face by saying yes to God and telling our brokenness to take a backseat. It took a few years, but two women learned that "almost free" wasn't freedom at all—or even close. It was simply the precursor to what was to come. The unfortunate truth is that we had to unpack a lifetime of emotional baggage in the spotlight of leadership. But instead of hiding it, we began to slowly shine a light on the things holding us captive.

Seven years later, I am more convinced than ever that God is still in the business of setting the captive free. I am who I am today because I let a few big-haired Southern girls go on this journey with me. In 2011 we founded Broken Girl Ministries, and today we don't even know who that broken girl is anymore. But one thing we do know: She's better than okay and is moving on.

We all have a story. Some are more messed up than others, but we all have one. Part of my story would make your head spin, but it's not really about what I have faced; it's about what happens after the breaking that deserves to be told, because God gets all of the credit and glory for that. I believe healing and freedom is not just about us. It's about all of the beautiful souls we take with us on this journey. Building healing community has been so important to me—not only in my writing and blogging, but also in my everyday life. I feel like this book was birthed out of healing sisterhood, so in 2018 I started a ministry called Tribal to connect women through mentoring. Freedom is something we do together in community, not just on our own.

Tribe: We're More Like a Small Gang

She was still small enough to carry, in first grade, and dealing with something her little mind couldn't process, or even verbalize. Her stress took on a different shape, one that looked like tears, a tummy ache, and even tired legs. My daughter's young teacher lovingly scooped her up and carried her to the nurse. This teacher wasn't a mother yet, but she stood in the gap for me to do what teachers do: They bend over backward and meet a need because of love, because this is what they've always wanted to do even though they are smart enough to be a doctor, or run a small country. They traded a big paycheck for little eyes that light up when they hear the smallest praise and the smell of sweaty kid, which smells kind of like a dog after a hard hour of play and picking wild flowers in the schoolyard.

When I arrived at the school, my firstborn was sleeping, mouth open and red-faced. One cheek was redder than the other. I scooped her up and carried her out, kissing her forehead and wondering what was wrong with my girl. Later, as she told me her symptoms, I listened, but she was peaceful and wasn't complaining anymore. God puts something special in moms, I think. It is a mixture of private eye and fiercely protective guard dog, but mostly it's selflessness. Maybe it's discernment and intuition; maybe it's listening to symptoms and trying to find a solution to kiss the hurt away. But later that night when it was time to tuck Whitley in, I asked if something was going on at school. Why was one side of her face, one spot in particular, red and swollen? What was causing it, and what happened?

She began to cry as she told me of two boys who circled her on the playground; they noticed the broken capillary on her face and pointed at it, making fun of the one tiny flaw. As they teased her they flicked her hard, in that same place, till it became more inflamed and blister-like. She sobbed, and I held her—and my breath—and listened closely to her words, feeling the sting she must have felt on her beautiful skin. She honestly never had cared about that spot on her face; the doctors said she would outgrow it, and when family members would point it out, wondering if she should have it *fixed*, she would say, "I just think it makes me . . . me." And I would smile proudly, wishing that I could be just like her and welcome flaws as gifts instead of highlighting them like those circling bullies who had exaggerated something barely noticeable into a head-turning disfigurement.

Words rained softly from my lips to comfort my girl, cloudy words that comforted me, as well, because I knew it was God in me being strong as I watched my girl feel so small. Her stiff body relaxed into me, into my words; she gave me a salty kiss and drifted to sleep. I cried and rocked her, whispering prayers over her and wishing her daddy were home instead of taking class at seminary a few hours away. Later, I was ticked. I slipped out of the place of comforting words, and salty prayers turned into a silent storm brewing that wanted to be loud thunder. I called her daddy, gave him the facts without tears or panic, and told him I was keeping her home, sending a long email with pictures of Whit's face, and taking care of it—and her.

His end was silent. I didn't like it. I needed his words. *Tell me I did a good job. Tell me the email was worded right and would be firm enough but from a heart that wanted it to be well-received*. But his silence looked like him wanting to jump in the car and come home. It also looked like holding two first-graders by the nape of the neck, with limbs dangling as he put the fear of God in them.

The situation was handled extremely well by the school, but mostly by a twenty-something teacher who was mad enough to make a room full of sweaty kids feel like they were in first-grade hell. While the class had a very bad day filled with lectures, Whitley and I had Mexican food with friends of mine who love her; they saw the mark on her face and smiled sad smiles, worrying about the possibility of a mark on her heart later. We shopped, and I bought her things she didn't need, trying to forget a moment that she didn't deserve, praying it would make the both of us stronger.

My girl is fifteen now, the broken capillary disappeared along with her small stature. She looks like a young woman, one who still needs a reminder to brush her hair and teeth. She still feels sick when dealing with something at school that makes her heart sad. She feels that anxious ache in the pit of her stomach, reminding her that something feels a little off. I'm still catching tears and saying wise words that come from something much bigger than me, and leaning on Whitley's amazing daddy to make sure I'm not stormy and unpredictable in trying to fix everything.

My girl still holds on to things until she can't anymore, and as she releases words and says, "I feel so much better," I feel like I'm going to vomit; but that passes, too. I definitely don't have it all figured out while I am bringing up my girls. My best friends don't have it all figured out while they are bringing up theirs. But the only thing I can think of that we are doing right is this: We are women who carry things that don't belong to us. We mother a child who isn't ours and scoop her up. We cry with a friend and don't blink when they swear like a sailor, followed by, "Will you pray for me?" We carry hearts and pain, not judgment.

We cradle our words carefully and beg God that somehow they will sound like His. This is hard stuff; none of us knows what we are doing. But we sure try hard. We hear words that haven't been said yet and feel the tears our brave friend cried the night before as she prayed to be seen mothering well in a world that makes us feel so invisible and small at times. We are women who carry things that are worth carrying, even if they are not our own. We are a force to be reckoned with, even with messy hearts. We post a guard and link arms until our girls are free and our prayers are answered.

And then we repeat this tug-of-war of carrying burdens, hoping to make them lighter, and trusting blindly in the God who teaches us how to lay them down at His feet for good this time. We aren't superheroes; we're more like a small gang. We carry things. We do not need praise, or position, or an award that highlights how stinkin' awesome we are. We are much too busy applauding others when they carry the hard things. And when we are weary and realize that needing others is actually the way that we love them in return, we take down our walls by allowing them to witness and love the weakest version of ourselves. And somehow we feel much better and really seen. We need each other and the power of community to walk in freedom.

> Carry each other's burdens, and in this way you will fulfill the law of Christ.
>
> Galatians 6:2

If You Are Doing This Alone, You're Doing It Wrong

In the last two weeks, major things have happened—good things and some heavy things, too. Isn't that how life works? You can have God-sized dreams happening and still hold on to them as though they could slip through your fingers like sand. Sometimes answered prayers are just as scary as delayed ones. Both require a change within if we are brave enough to face the fears that hold us back. There are two sides of me: the awkward-introvert side that spills things and feels anxiety in large crowds, and the gutsy side that says, "So, hey, I need time with you to ask you a million questions because I trust your advice. I trust you."

It's kind of crazy, right, to reach out to others? It's pretty gutsy and bold. Because of my history with people-pleasing, I tend to give people easy outs due to lingering trust issues because in the past I was disappointed in adults who lacked follow-through. In this case, what I have to work with is a recipe for keeping things easier to handle on my own because it's less chaotic and doesn't make me emotional. Mix in a history dealing with verbal abuse and a tiny dose of physical abuse, and you have a girl who isn't really great at asking for help. I was independent because I had to be. I played it safe.

But *safe* isn't very fun. Playing it safe out of fear is the most isolating thing you can do. If you ask me when real spiritual and personal growth happened in my life, I will tell you it was when I let others mentor me and even mother me a little. They invested in me first; I looked at their character and their life and said, "Okay, I'll let you in. But you have to let me in, too." That is freaking scary, am I right?

In the past, to me, asking for help meant weakness. But because of the wholeness I have found in Christ, I know He is my source; He alone supplies all my needs. Whole people let others in. *Yeah, that only took me a few decades to learn. I'm still bad at it but I'm growing.* If we want greatness in our lives, we have to surround ourselves with women and men who are doing life well, and who are smarter and wiser than we are. Jesus will be your source, and we can be a tribe of women who help others heal, instead of wounding them.

I experienced a real breakthrough after years of being personally stuck and stifled, but now I am living beyond the breakthrough, beyond the breaking. I am walking in wholeness, and that's what I want for you more than anything. If I can do this, anyone can do this, because God loves you just as much as He loves me. Reaching out and being still enough to allow others to speak into my life has been solid gold. Who actually makes the time to talk on the phone with someone they don't know very well when they sound a little panicky? Women who invest in other women, that's who.

And what kind of man says, "I don't know why I am telling you all this, but I know that it's the Holy Spirit," and then tells you to make a list of what fuels you and drains you and gives you the best advice ever? Like, who says you don't have to be good at everything? Good men, lovingly referred to as Pops and pillars in the church, that's who. We grow by letting others into our lives, being vulnerable, and asking important questions.

"What are your guidelines, so to speak, for women's ministry and mentoring?"

When a lady asked me that, this was my response: To support women to their face and behind their back. Two-sided mentoring, where women give and not just take. Mentoring where you look at that younger woman fully convinced she has just as much to offer you, and you have so much to offer her, as well. Be confident in that. You listen, really listen. You are positive and kind; you make deposits before you make withdrawals.

You should be drawn to the older woman who is wiser and smarter than you, and you listen to her. Glean from her and remind her why her voice is one women like you need to hear. Celebrate her, and don't you dare phase her out. You need her more than ever. Mentoring is about growth and connection, never dissension.

I'm so over gossip as prayer requests. Let's call it what it is and call it out. We all need to be better at this. Let's give men a reason to stop calling women crazy. And, if by chance, we are acting crazy, we must ask ourselves if it is because we are mad and fed up because the wrong voices are magnified and loud while we've been quiet, slow to speak, and have been taught to play it safe and small instead of starting a fire-filled revival where hearts are changed and women are safe. Get mad and fight *for* your girls, not *with* them. Speak the truth in love because you know you are loved and you want to love well, not because you want to prove a point or be in the right.

My passion with Tribal is biblical mentoring—Titus 2:3–5 stuff. It's so simple, really, and basic. And yet it's been complicated with "shoulds" and personal preference and to tell you the truth, I've hated it sometimes and wanted nothing to do with it. Women crave connection, so let's make sure it's godly and healthy instead of worldly and toxic. Godly and toxic don't go together because the fruits of the Spirit are beautiful and lovely and warm and inviting.

Lead with honesty, integrity, and vulnerability. Go back to the basics. Free your heart from frustration with the older or younger generation—none of us truly knows everything, and that's okay because we are following the One who does. Jesus never, ever talked down to women. Ever. He praised the Gentile woman for her crumb-hungry faith and answered her prayers and healed her daughter (Matthew 15:28).

A few years ago at a Saving Grace banquet, Mary DeMuth was the speaker. Something she said has stayed with me from that moment on: *"Good community heals bad community."*

I believe healing sisterhood is supposed to be the good community that heals the bad, not the other way around. Sure, I'm forty-two and fiery—so I've been told many times. I'll charge hell with a water pistol, sure. But I've also been the held-back one, shy, and scared to look you in the eye because I know what abuse looks like and I know when I feel safe. If you have lost your fire, I'll share some of mine with you. If you've forgotten what you have to offer and that we all need you, I'll be the first one in line to remind you.

But if you are a mean girl, heal first before you try to lead others. Please heal, and let God do the work that only He can do inside of you. We need you and we need you whole. You are not a lost cause. You are ready for something new and for God to do a new thing in you.

It's time for women to lead well and create a safe place for other women. You in? Because that's what women are waiting on. Be soft and strong, Spirit-led and fiery. Be who God called you to be and don't be scared of what that looks like and if you don't fit.

You Fit. You Belong. Believe That.

For the past two years, I have been simplifying my life. It has been wonderful. It's little things like deleting LinkedIn and even deleting a few people and connections on social media who have repeatedly broken trust and bashed people who I love. I know this world is not nice, and I try hard to be kind and loving, but it's super important to unsubscribe from unnecessary drama. If that means "friends" and even family have "deleted" me, then I'm really all for it. I want people to experience lasting freedom and breakthrough spiritually. When you see the picture of *that* person pop up in your feed, you have to deal with all the things that flood your heart. Whether it's lust, regret, or just being ticked off. If that means forgiving someone a million times until it sticks, do it for your heart. If it means forgiving yourself, do it. Release it. Move on. Don't be a victim or invite a victim mentality to become how you process everything. You are stronger than you think. Your heart is worthy of protecting.

We can love people face-to-face in a way that brings God glory and heals old wounds. You can be the hands and feet of Jesus to this world without having everyone "like" you and "follow" you. Being a real friend is more important. Invest in those life-giving friendships and relationships. Partner with people who are truth-speakers and not pot-stirrers.

If you are a leader and no one is following, it might not be the followers' fault. If I am speaking and everyone wants to hit the mute button, that's on me. Seriously. Be loyal. Be real. Be kind. Heal. Love. Forgive. Repeat. And if you need to, delete, delete, delete. You are precious. You are worth it. You are enough. Guard that heart of yours, okay, but love yourself enough to take walls down that have kept you isolated from the right people.

A friend of mine shared a quote with me: "To know you is to love you, and if they don't love you, then they don't know you." Maybe they don't know you, maybe they do. Maybe you don't know you, or don't even know how to love yourself. Maybe it's time to try again.

Repeat after me: I'm not a big deal, but I'm a big deal to God and to the people who love me.

Mothering Mentors, the Heartbeat of Tribal

I have always been captivated by the story of Ruth and Naomi. Maybe it's the mentoring-mothering connection and that at different parts of this story these women take turns nurturing one another. Maybe it's because it is about two women from different generations who desperately need each other, but only one of them seems to know it at first. Sometimes the people we need most are the people we try to push away when our heart is hurting.

In Ruth 1:19, the wounded widow returns home without sons, without her love, and without hope for provision. Naomi's pain left her almost unrecognizable, yet her people saw traces of the woman they used to know. She went out full and came home empty (v. 21). But she did not return alone. Clinging to her side and the God she served stood the devoted daughter-in-law who refused to leave her stranded in her sorrow. Ruth made a vow to the broken mother: "Where you die, I will die. And there will I be buried. The Lord do so to me, and more also, if anything but death parts you and me" (Ruth 1:17 NKJV).

Home was wherever they stood. Together. Broken. In need. Hungry. Clinging to a thread of hope and each other. We were never meant to do this thing called life on our own. Love doesn't walk out on you when all of life gives way and crumbles; it stands with you even though you tell it to go away. You may feel like you have nothing to offer in a state of brokenness, but with all my heart I believe that letting people love you and loving them back means a complete willingness to show them our "ugly." We shouldn't have to jump through invisible hoops in hopes of earning love, but we do. We jump through hoops. We go through the motions. We fake it trying to mask the pain.

When Naomi spilled out her bitter complaint, blaming the very God who gave her a determined daughter, I see no reply of reproach or index finger in her face, just a hand to hold as they return to a land at the beginning of the harvest season. A quiet presence walking with her through the hurt, Ruth steps in to nurture Naomi and work another man's land to provide for her. Ruth works hard and finds herself content with leftovers. She proves herself a virtuous woman, and the people take notice. The kinsman redeemer takes notice of her and rewards her. Gleaning for leftovers turns into prosperity, wedding bells, sounds of babies crying, and second chances.

The God we serve does not give us leftovers. He goes all out with the full spread. He prepares a table for us in the presence of our enemies. He fills our cups until they overflow as goodness and mercy follow us. Not just on certain days, but all of our days (Psalm 23:5–6). His is the hand we want to hold, and He is the friend who walks with us through the mess. So work the land, cry your tears, but give God your broken today and your hopeful tomorrow. Let the bitterness spill out in salty form and pray until it's emptied out.

> Then the women said to Naomi, "Blessed be the Lord, who has not left you this day without a close relative; and may his name be famous in Israel! And may he be to you a restorer of life and a nourisher of your old age; for your daughter-in-law, who loves you, who is better to you than seven sons, has borne him."
>
> Ruth 4:14–15 NKJV

I am overwhelmed with gratitude for the hands I get to hold along this journey. I feel like that devoted daughter who says "till death do we part." I want to be better than seven sons, diligently working with these soft hands and soft heart while my God takes notice. We take turns nurturing the generations, loving them, tending to them, and listening when our Naomis offer instructions on how to live, grieve, and return back to a place of hopefulness. Find your Naomi and adopt her. Find your Ruth and let her be a little clingy at times. We need each other, we really do.

Truth You (and Your Tribe) Need

You don't have to show up perfect, you just have to show up. You are needed.

You need a tribe; we are not meant to walk through life alone. Freedom is something we live together, not just on our own. It's time to stop hiding. It's time for our breakthrough. It's time to take hold of what God promises us—freedom!

Reflective Question

My final question for you, beloved: Are you part of a healing community? If not, I pray that you find one and join it!

Gutsy Prayer

Lord,

I pray for my sister reading this prayer. More than anything I want her to know how loved she is and how much this world needs what she has to offer. I pray that this is just the beginning of her Freedom! journey and that you will increase her confidence in you and who you have created her to be. I pray that she will feel you near, know that she is Holy Spirit–empowered because you dwell in her (1 Corinthians 3:16). She is a warrior with a soft heart and hands. She is a royal priesthood, a holy nation, your very own special possession (1 Peter 2:9). Bless her beyond her wildest dreams and awaken her for MORE of you!

In Jesus' name, amen.

Epilogue

WHAT A JOURNEY this has been for me. I am so honored that you have been on it with me. When you write a book about freedom and breakthrough, you can be sure that the enemy will try to stand in the way and keep you not only from writing the book of your dreams, but living the heart of the message. In the past three months alone, I have said good-bye to two precious family members, both tragic losses for our family. But one of them has been far harder on my family's heart: Last week we laid to rest my beautiful stepsister, Christie, who was only forty-three. I felt this message awaken in my heart like never before for the hearts of women. And I experienced a need for a breakthrough of my own to continue to step out in faith to do the things God has asked me to in this season.

Life doesn't stop turning when we go through hard things, but during this time of loss I had a peace so real that I have been able to face each day and show up for life with a gutsy faith that trusted God would take care of everything my family was facing.

Something beautiful happened in March when I launched "Tribal: Connecting Like-Hearts to Jesus and Other Women Through Mentoring": Floods of women contacted me from all over the U.S., asking how they could be a part of something like it. Now more than ever, women are hungry for real connection with other women of like faith. They are longing for freedom, and they want someone to experience it with. It's up to us to live this message of *Freedom!* and to invite others on this journey with us. I know breakthrough and freedom are possible because I am living them with a group of tribal soul sisters both near and far. This hasn't been just a process of writing a book—it's been an answer to a call to start Tribal and make sure this becomes something women can develop in their churches and communities. I can't wait to see what you do, you gutsy girl. Welcome to the tribe. I am so glad we found each other.

Love you like crazy,
Jennifer Renee

Acknowledgments

I DON'T KNOW WHAT I DID to deserve so many incredible people in my life, but I'm truly thankful for each one of you. Women and readers whom I have never met before have become my tribe, my long-distance community, as well as my inspiration for writing about breakthrough and freedom. I hope I get to meet you and hug all of your necks someday because I truly love you.

To my husband, Jonathan, you have been my rock, my constant support, the taxi driver for our girls, and my personal takeout delivery man. You have gone above and beyond to support me while I have been writing this book. You made so many sacrifices to see me get to this point—thank you from the bottom of my heart. I love you. I am grateful for you, and I am so glad you are my Baby Daddy.

To my daughters, Whitley and Elise, you light my little world on fire and bring me so much joy. Being your mom is the highlight of my life, my greatest joy, and the best thing I will ever do in life. I love you more.

I could not have done any of this without my agent and friend, Blythe Daniel. You, friend, are a gift. Your belief in me and guidance has been a treasure that I will be forever grateful for. Thank you.

To all my family, especially my mom, heart daddy, and baby sister, Carrie. Thank you for loving me always. You mean the world to me.

And to my acquisitions editor, Kim Bangs. I will forever love you for the way you fought for me for a really, really long time. Thank you for being my fellow warrior and inspiring me to write this and giving me a big kick in the pants when I needed it. You are one of my favorite gutsy girls.

To Sharon Hodge, my editor and miracle worker, I cannot thank you enough for your passion, skill, and the way you encouraged me throughout this entire process. Thank you for bringing out the very best in me.

To my soul sister, Holley, thank you for sitting beside me in a cute little coffee shop and keeping me company while I wrote this book. You have been my sweetest cheerleader.

To Keri and Bridgette, thank you for being part of my healing sisterhood.

To ALL my friends and tribe who have cheered me on every step of this journey. I want so much to list every single one of you, but if I tried it would take days. But you know who you are. You are my tribe and my soul sisters, ride or die, or sit and snack. . . . I love you so much I can hardly stand it. Thank you for loving me, making me laugh, and talking me off of multiple ledges. Forget that it takes a village, tribes get stuff DONE.

I'm so grateful for my church family in Bella Vista and my incredible students who have prayed for me and loved me. I love all of you dearly.

And to my first and truest love, Jesus, thank you for setting this broken girl free. Until there are no broken girls, I'm in for whatever.

Notes

Chapter 3: Taking It Back: The Same Kind of Stuck

1. Jack W. Hayford, ed., *Spirit-Filled Life Bible NKJV, A Personal Study Bible Unveiling All God's Fullness In All God's Word* (Nashville: Thomas Nelson, 1991), 306.

Chapter 6: Freedom from Your Inner Mean Girl

1. Charles Swindoll, *Encourage Me: Caring Words for Heavy Hearts* (Grand Rapids, MI: Zondervan, 1993), 72.
2. Brené Brown, *Daring Greatly: How the Courage to Be Vulnerable Transforms the Way We Live, Love, Parent, and Lead* (New York: Avery, 2012), 10.
3. Holley Gerth, *Fiercehearted: Live Fully, Love Bravely* (Grand Rapids, MI: Revell, 2017), 69.
4. William Congreve, *The Mourning Bride*, 1697.

Chapter 7: The Mending Mindset: Reclaim Your Role as the Leading Lady

1. *The Holiday*, directed by Nancy Meyers (Los Angeles: Columbia Pictures, 2006), DVD.
2. *The Holiday*, DVD.
3. "Gumption," Macmillan Dictionary, https://www.macmillandictionary.com/us/dictionary/american/gumption.

Chapter 8: The Price of Breakthrough

1. Becky Shaffer, "Addressing Those On the Front Line of Our Failing Child Welfare System," God's Grateful Girl's Blog, May 14, 2011, www.godsgratefulgirl.wordpress.com/2011/05/14.

2. Melissa Blair, "A Letter to My Sixteen Year Old Self on Her Abortion," Melissablair.net, http://melissablair.net/letter-sixteen-year-old-self-abortion/.

Chapter 9: You Are the Catalyst to the Breakthrough You Are Looking For

1. *Wonder Woman*, directed by Patty Jenkins (Burbank, CA: Warner Brothers, 2017), DVD.

Chapter 10: Beyond the Breakthrough

1. Holley Gerth, *You're Loved No Matter What: Freeing Your Heart from the Need to Be Perfect* (Grand Rapids, MI: Revell, 2015), 11.

Chapter 11: Abundantly More, Ending our Tug-of-War with Joy

1. "Dr. Brené Brown On Joy: It's Terrifying," *SuperSoul Sunday*, OWN Network, March 17, 2013, https://www.dialogues.org/interview/03/17/2013/dr-brene-brown-on-joy-it-s-terrifying-supersoul-sunday-oprah-winfrey-network/1483231368.

2. Brené Brown, *The Gifts of Imperfection: Let Go of Who You Think You're Supposed to Be and Embrace Who You Are* (Center City, MN: Hazelden, 2010), 79.

3. "Brené Brown Breaks Down Common Types of Armor," *Oprah's Lifeclass*, Oprah Winfrey Network, October 6, 2013, https://www.youtube.com/watch?v=ht5dDInnTzM.

4. Brown, *Oprah's Lifeclass*.

Jennifer Renee Watson is a pastor's wife, youth minister, mother of two teenagers, author, blogger, and speaker who believes normal is overrated. She is the founder of "Tribal: Connecting Like-Hearts to Jesus and Other Women Through Mentoring," and has a passion for connecting the generations and leading women to experience lasting freedom in their lives. You can connect with Jennifer Renee at www.jenniferreneewatson.com.